CW00495145

IT'S A WEIRD WORLD

When we first asked readers to send in letters to *Fortean Times* magazine concerning their more unusual experiences, little did we suspect that they would become the basis of a series that now, with this latest instalment, reaches its fifth volume!

Perhaps, though, we shouldn't be surprised. We all have a need to share our stories – especially the weird ones. And, equally, we all love to hear other peoples' accounts of the strangest things that have ever happened to them. Some of these tales are amusing, some just a wee bit odd. Some are vaguely unsettling, disturbing even, and remind us that for all our faith in a predictable everyday reality – the one in which we get up and go to work each day and do the weekly shop at the supermarket – the world has a habit of turning distinctly odd or slightly surreal every once in a while. And then there are the stories – best read at night, perhaps, by the light of a flickering candle – which send a shiver down the spine and make you look nervously over your shoulder...

You'll find examples of all these within these pages – from a baffling encounter with a man dressed as a giant rabbit to a terrifying run-in with a violent poltergeist. Not to mention accounts of hauntings, pre-monitions, time-slips, teleportations and weird old ladies.

And new mysteries are constantly popping up to surprise and spook us, like the numerous baffling cases of Dog-Headed Men and scary Shadow People that we present here for the first time.

We hope you enjoy this latest bulletin from the world of the weird, and that you'll find the time to share your own strange stories and uncanny experiences with us – see page 161 to find out how you can tell us that It Happened to You...

David Sutton, Editor, *Fortean Times*

It Happened To Me!

REAL-LIFE TALES OF THE PARANORMAL
VOLUME 5

Ordinary people's extraordinary stories from
the pages of FORTEAN TIMES

EDITED AND COMPILED BY
David Sutton

PHOTOGRAPHY AND DESIGN
Etienne Gilfillan

COVER IMAGE
David Sutton/Abigail Mason/Etienne Gilfillan

PUBLISHING & MARKETING
Paul Rayner
020 7907 6663
paul_rayner@dennis.co.uk

MAGBOOK PUBLISHER
Dharmesh Mistry
020 7907 6100
dharmesh_mistry@dennis.co.uk

MAG**BOOK**

To syndicate content from this product
please contact Anj Dosaj-Halai on
+44 (0) 20 7907 6132 or email
anj_dosaj-halai@dennis.co.uk

LIABILITY
While every care was taken during
the production of this MagBook, the
publishers cannot be held responsible
for the accuracy of the information or
any consequence arising from it. Dennis
Publishing takes no responsibility for the
companies advertising in this MagBook.
The paper used within this MagBook
is produced from sustainable fibre,
manufactured by mills with a valid chain of
custody. Printed at Stones.

It Happened To Me!

REAL-LIFE TALES OF THE PARANORMAL
VOLUME FIVE

ORDINARY PEOPLE'S EXTRAORDINARY
STORIES FROM THE PAGES OF FORTEAN TIMES

CONTENTS

1 *It's About Time...*

Strange phenomena involving apparent slips, warps and tears in the fabric of time are among the most intriguing on record – like the classic 'Versailles time-slip' in which two English ladies found themselves apparently transported back to the days of Marie Antoinette. While there turns out to be a rational explanation for the first story in our collection, some of the others remain genuinely baffling...

TIME-SLIPS

SHEFFIELD 'TIME-SLIP'

I had an experience that could have ended up being the British equivalent of the famous Ghosts of Versailles time-slip. In the 1990s, I was lecturing at Sheffield Hallam University and living opposite the General Cemetery. Opened in 1836, this was the main burial ground of Victorian Sheffield and is awash with Greek Doric and Egyptian-style tombs.

One morning while walking through the cemetery on my way to work, I was brought up short by the sight of a woman dressed in Victorian mourning dress. She was deep in conversation with a man wearing Victorian tailoring and a top hat. Feverishly, my mind tried to make sense of what I was seeing. I even closed my eyes to see if the two figures would disappear when I reopened them – they didn't. Within seconds, I was already thinking in terms of ghosts or a time-slip, and if I hadn't gritted my teeth and kept walking towards the couple I am sure this is the explanation I would have come to.

However, as I got closer another woman appeared and approached the two figures. She was dressed in modern-day clothing and was holding a clipboard. The sight of a camera led to a paradigm shift in my understanding of what I was seeing. When I reached the two Victorian figures, who were very much flesh and blood, I said: "You have just nearly given me a heart attack!" They laughed and explained they were making an amateur film about the cemetery.

There are several things I gathered from this experience, which I think may have a bearing on the Ghosts of Versailles story. Firstly, like the Misses Moberly and Jourdain, I already knew a lot about the location. In fact, I used the cemetery as a teaching aid in lectures, so was already 'primed' with an historical context into which I could fit the two apparently anomalous figures. Secondly, as someone with an interest in strange phenomena, I was also predisposed to consider a supernatural explanation and my mind brought the categories of 'ghosts' and 'time-slip' almost immediately to the top of my 'possible definitions' list. Finally, if I had not approached the 'Victorians' and had turned and headed in the other direction, I would probably have settled on the time-slip explanation and dined out on it ever since.

Paul Walker, Billingham, Cleveland, 2011

DAZED EXPLORERS

When my mum was about 20, in the late 1960s, she was in a really busy tube station in the centre of London in winter. Amongst the crowd were a man and woman, dressed in safari suits – the kind people wore early last century.

OK, I hear you say, there could be plenty of explanations for that. But what really struck my mum was the expressions on their faces – and this has stayed with her to this day. They looked really dazed. Not confused in the way a foreigner in a busy tube station may look, but completely dazed. They had no luggage, and their clothes were not suited to the winter. My mum described it as if they had literally been picked up and put there. The other weird thing is that she looked around to check other peoples' reactions, but nobody else seemed to be looking at them.

I accept there could be many rational explanations, but for this to stay with her so vividly for so many years makes me wonder if there was something paranormal about it – a time-slip perhaps? Or an abduction, with the victims put back in the wrong time/place?

Anon, Fortean Times Message Board (FTMB), 2004

AVEBURY VISION

Several years ago, I was visiting Avebury. We stayed at a private house, the guest bedroom of which was practically intersected by the main stone circle.

“ *I was standing in front of the window, looking out into the night at the stones* ”

From the outset, I felt disquieted by the atmosphere in the house – the owner was a rather strange person, and there was a rather unpleasant feeling all round. We felt disinclined to spend too much time there, so spent most of the evening in the pub.

We repaired to bed at around 11, tipsy but certainly not inordinately drunk. At around two or three in the morning, I woke up with a start, and felt compelled to go over to the window and look outside. To my great surprise, I seemed to be looking out onto a sunlit day. I could see three distinct characters dressed in 1930s hiking clothes – a youngish man and woman and what appeared to be their son, wandering around the stones, as if on a jolly Sunday outing.

Suddenly, the image vanished, and I realised that I was standing in front of the window, but looking out into the night at the stones, with the branches of a tree tapping eerily at the window. There was no one in sight. It was certainly the most vivid and lifelike "dream" that I had ever had. I wouldn't have given it any more thought if I had simply woken up in bed having had such a dream. But to wake up and find myself standing bodily at the same window was a very curious sensation, especially as I have never been prone to somnambulism. I have often wondered what this strange experience might have meant.
Lise Cribbin, Munich, Germany, 2010

TEDDY BOY TIME-SLIP
Back in 1979, when I was about 10 years old, my parents took my sister and I for a day trip to the Essex countryside. On the way home we passed through a small

village. My dad drove down a one-way street and came to a T-junction which was obstructed by a large American car. It was a hideous 'psychedelic' purplish colour (almost like the rainbow effect you see on the back of a CD) but obviously well looked after, judging by the acres of highly polished chrome. I have never seen a car with such an unusual paint job, before or since.

The driver, a middle-aged man with the most absurd boot-polish black DA haircut, and his partner, with an equally out-of-place beehive hairdo, were standing outside the car. He was wearing a yellow 'teddy boy' outfit and she a 1950s-style skirt and blouse. They had spread a tablecloth over the roof of their vehicle and had assembled a pretty large picnic on it. I remember plates and plates of exotic-looking food – much, much more than you would imagine for just two people, and not just cheese and pickle sarnies – and a bottle of champagne in a cooler. These guys were just eating their dinner in the middle of the road without a care in the world.

There were parked cars down both sides of the street and this car was blocking the whole road. There was no way around them. My dad leant out the window and asked them what they thought they were doing. The guy responded that his car had broken down and that "we have called in the army", which struck us all as a bit odd and was probably why my dad left it at that.

So we backed the car up about 50 ft (15m) and turned into another road. Less than 30 seconds later we were passing the intersection, fully expecting to see the car and its owners enjoying their picnic, but car, picnic and owners had completely disappeared.

Even if their car had been working properly, I fail to see how they could have packed up their massive picnic and driven off in the very short time it took for us to take our detour. My dad was incredulous and for a moment we thought we had come out on a different road, but we recognised the antique and bike shops on the corner. We drove around for a bit but couldn't see any sign of the car or its strange occupants.

It's a mystery that has puzzled us to this day.
Anon, FTMB, 2004

WARTIME WATERLOO

Back in May or June of 1992, I experienced what I can only think was a time slip. I had gone up to London with a new boyfriend, and we caught a train to Waterloo and then headed down into the underground. I can't remember which entrance we took: I just remember heading down the escalators and seeing scraps of paper lazily blow past me up the other way. That was the first hint of weirdness. The paper wasn't gusting like it normally would in the blast of subway air – this looked like slow motion.

It was at that point that I think I sensed the shift in atmosphere. From the normally bustling energy of Waterloo on a Saturday, it segued into a heavier, depressing gloom. Everything was too quiet. Even though there were still people around, they all seemed subdued. It was almost like being underwater.

At the foot of the escalators, there were lines and lines of string, like multitudes of washing lines. Bits of cloth and rag were hung up on the lines, as though makeshift camps had been set up all along corridors and in any available space. It wasn't just a couple of isolated areas – it felt as if all the passages had been turned into living areas or camps. I don't remember which underground line we were taking, but we seemed to be walking a lot farther than usual. The strangest thing was, I felt so tense and at a gut level knew that the surroundings had flipped into something more alien, yet it never occurred to me to say something to my boyfriend.

Standing in a corner was a man in official uniform – I don't really remember him, just have a sense that he was bareheaded with shiny buttons on his jacket – whose presence made me feel no less uneasy. I was trying to convince myself that if he were there, it meant that all the weirdness of the clotheslines was somehow explicable. Only afterwards, when my boyfriend and I compared notes, did we realise that we both sensed something archaic about his outfit and demeanour.

By the time I got on the semi-crowded tube train, I was beginning to feel seriously panicked. Sitting across from us was a man who looked close to tears, red faced, breathing frantically, a really scared expression on his face. My boyfriend gave a surreptitious nod in his direction – the first clue that I wasn't the only one experiencing something disquieting. Then my boyfriend whispered, "Look, him too," and I saw another man further down the carriage who looked in fear of his life. At that point, it still didn't occur to us to wonder what the hell was going on – we just both thought that maybe we'd had a premonition or something and ought to get off the train immediately. Only afterwards did we realise it had felt totally strange from the moment we headed down into the underground station. I guess we both assume that perhaps it was some kind of time slip back to what might have been the Second World War – I don't know if they turned any parts of Waterloo Station into air raid shelters.

It's not as dramatic as hanging out with Marie Antoinette in Versailles, but it still creeped me out big time, and whenever I think about it I still recall just how scared it made me.

Laragh Rogers, by email, 2005

THYME SLIP

As my partner and I approached the ruins of Netley Abbey near Southampton, about 5m (16ft) away from the first walls, we both noticed a strong smell of thyme and mentioned it to each other straight away. We were not anywhere near the shrubbery and the smell was contained in about a 2 sq m (22 sq ft) area. Could it have once been a herb garden, the smell slipping through time? Well, maybe...

Brian Hopkins, Southsea, Hampshire, 2011

WARPS IN TIME?

SPECTRAL REWINDING

While sitting in a cafe in Covent Garden last summer, I noticed out of the corner of my eye across the street what appeared to be a man walking backwards. I looked again more attentively, but saw nothing. During the course of my hot chocolate I kept a close eye on the spot where I had seen the figure, and about five minutes later I saw him again.

Nobody else seemed aware of the 'person'; he seemed solid and real, but disappeared again after about 40 seconds. He again walked backwards, and seemed to be wearing a suit from the 1950s. He gave me the impression of 'flickering' in and out of existence. I kept watch in the hope of a third sighting, but with no luck. I wondered if this could be a ghostly recording 'rewinding'. We hear about spectral images playing out past events, but surely they must rewind too?

James Laurent Toure, by email, 2000

TAKE TWO

One recent hot summer's day, I was cycling my usual circuit, which takes in

Hurley Lock on the Thames. I had just entered the lock from a path on the weir side. As I stopped and reached for a drink, I watched the lock keeper on the other bank, walking to the upstream end of the lock to open the gates. He was wearing a distinctive brown hat and waved and shouted to someone. As he got to the gate control, I took a swig of water, and because of the sun's glare I shut my eyes. My world went 'wibble' at this point and I felt a little dizzy for a second or two, not unusual after a workout and then stopping. When I lowered my water bottle, there once again was the lock keeper, replaying the same walk, wave and shout. I am certain that in the couple of seconds I was distracted, he couldn't have returned to the downstream gate and started again. I felt very odd for several minutes afterwards. Is Hurley known for peculiar time-keeping?
Steve Small, by email, 2010

THE LOST HOUR

I lost an hour of my life. It was 14 years ago – I was 17 – but I can still remember the events of that day with the clarity of a recent event. I had cycled out into the countryside to visit a school friend. He lived in a village on the Severn estuary and the late March winds made the ride a slow and tedious plough. It was overcast and didn't look like it would get any nicer as the day went on.

The house was around 200 years old, a butcher's and baker's that had been knocked through to make one building. It stood on a crossroads; on the opposite side of the road was a cottage with a shop within that also doubled as the local Post Office. Although there was an operational nuclear power station within two miles of the village, it still seemed remote and untouched by the modern world. A hundred yards from the crossroads was an abandoned shop festooned with tin signs for bygone products such as Mazawatee tea. It was locked up and hadn't been entered for 15 years.

An old man had run the shop with his sister, and when she died he had locked up and moved in with his brother a couple of miles up the road, never to return or allow anyone to go inside the building. My friend and I would peer through the dusty windows at the shelves lined with long defunct products in their sun-bleached boxes.

On the day in question we spent the morning smoking cigarettes, drinking coffee and listening to records. It was a very normal morning; nothing really happened. Neither of us drove at that stage and living in a rural area we felt trapped by our surroundings, there never seemed to be anything to do. It was cold and wet, so when we wanted to smoke we had to go into an old out-building that had once been the abattoir.

At one o'clock – I remember the time because we wanted to make sure that we were back in time to watch Kimberly Davies on *Neighbours* – we decided to head over to the shop to get some lunch. Just as we were about to leave, the telephone rang. It was my friend's mother. They talked for a minute or so and then she had to go; she worked in a travel agent's and a customer had come in. They agreed that she would call back after five minutes when we had got back from the shop.

Outside, the crossroads was thick with fog, something not all that unusual in the village. What was unusual, however, was that the fog had a green tinge to it. We stood and looked up at the mist for a minute or so and decided that the green light must be coming from the power station. Inside the shop we bought pasties, crisps and cans of drinks, spoke briefly to the lady behind the counter, and then headed back across the road to my friend's house. In total we cannot have been gone for more than 10 minutes.

We walked back inside the house to the sound of the telephone ringing. It was my friend's mother and I could hear her voice shouting down the phone as soon as he picked up the hand set. Where had we been, she wanted to know; she had been calling for the past hour. My friend's face at first showed indignation but then, when he noticed the clock on the wall, it turned to bafflement. It was indeed an hour later. She didn't believe us of course, and thought we'd been up to no good. In fact she got even angrier when she heard our justification, cross that we'd try and fool her with such an unlikely story.

We went through to the living room and switched the television on. The programme showing was the one after the one after *Neighbours*. We didn't know how to react. We were numb, I think; confused more than anything else, but I think that we were also a bit scared, although neither of us wanted to show that to the other. We had absolutely no explanation for what had happened. There had been no 'blank' or 'dark' period that we were aware of during our trip across the road. Any time that had been lost – if indeed that had happened – had been lost 'seamlessly'.

After we got back to school we mentioned what had happened to a few friends. No one believed us. As a result both of us stopped talking about it to other people. When we meet up now we occasionally go over what happened on that day and try and come up with rational explanations, and when that inevita-

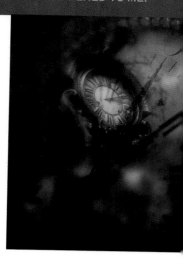

> ❝ *Any time that had been lost – if that had happened – had been lost seamlessly* ❞

bly fails we try to avoid looking for more the more outlandish explanations that readily spring to mind.

The house no longer belongs to my friend's family, the shop is now just a cottage, and the other shop, the one frozen in time, has now been bought by someone escaping city life, and its contents have been removed. My friend and I are no closer to understanding where that hour went, and I don't suppose we ever shall be.

Matthew Davey, by email, 2010

TIME-WARPED FRIEND?

Sometime in late 1999 or early 2000, a few friends and I had a get-together. We had recently finished university and were at one of my friends' parents' house while they were away. Earlier, we had all been sitting out on the garden patio, but it had got dark and cold and we had all moved into the lounge. I decided to go outside for a cigarette, so left the lounge and went through the kitchen and sat on a patio chair just outside the back door. Straight ahead was a path up the garden and to the side, halfway up the garden, was a greenhouse that had been converted into a summerhouse. One of my friends had gone up to it and had a smoke in it earlier on, just for the novelty value. (It wasn't warm this time of year, but he didn't have such facilities in his own garden).

So, I was sitting peacefully outside the back door peering out into the dark when I heard the downstairs lavatory (just off the kitchen) flush and my friend walked past the back door on his way back to the lounge. He walked out past me and I grunted some kind of hello and watched as he walked up the garden path and opened the door of the greenhouse and went in. "What's he going up there again for, at this time of night?" I thought. It was late and cold, but it wasn't out of character for him to act on some whim to go and explore the garden again at such a house-do.

I finished my cigarette and went back through the kitchen to the lounge, only to find all of my friends present and correct, including the bloke who was supposed to be in the greenhouse. I was speechless with shock for a few moments, before I demanded incredulously how the hell he had done that, since there was no other way into the house except the front door on the other side of the building. It would have taken much longer to get even half way there than for me to stroll through the kitchen. He was as bewildered as me and it was only when I refused to calm down and had gone through everything two or three times that everyone began to realise that I wasn't joking.

My friend had indeed been to the lavatory, but had not come out into the garden, simply gone straight back into the lounge. By now we were all a little spooked, but plucked up the courage to go and have a look outside. Of course, there was no one in the greenhouse, and no one anywhere else in the garden.

My only hypothesis is that as he had passed the open back door on the way back from the lavatory, at which point I had grunted a hello, the familiar situation had triggered a memory playback in my brain. I had been sitting in that exact chair in that exact position earlier on in the evening, when the same friend had come out of the back door and gone up to the greenhouse the first time.

I have heard that experiments during brain surgery have shown it possible to trigger playback of memories as if they are actually happening, and am also aware that certain unique smells, for example, can trigger very precise memories not possible to recall otherwise. Given the right circumstances and stimuli, can one trigger a flashback of recent memory? Or is this indeed some kind of phantom of the living, time warp or glitch in reality?

Tom Morton, by email, 2010

TRAIN PREVIEW

One Monday morning in 2004 I was on my way to Peterborough for a training course. I had to change trains several times and, as is almost always the case, missed my connection from Grantham station by seconds.

I checked when the next train was due and went to sit at the platform to wait. As time went on I became more and more anxious, not wanting to be late on my first day and make a bad impression. Eventually, three minutes before it was due, I saw the train coming round the bend (about 200 metres from where I was standing). I noticed that it was a very pretty train (as far as they go); it was blue and yellow, much like the old British Rail trains, but had a pointed nose and looked very modern.

I was incredibly relieved and stood and walked to the front of the platform. When I got there, I looked up, expecting to see the train almost right in front of me, but it wasn't there. Nor was there a train anywhere around the platforms. Slightly bemused by this, I returned to my seat. Two and a half minutes later, I again looked up to see the exact same scene as before, the same train coming around the bend. Thankfully, this time it arrived at the platform.

Other than a handful of experiences of déjà vu, this is the first time I've ever seen something before it's happened. What I'd like to ask is, now that I've had one premonition, am I likely to get more of them?

Anon, FTMB, 2004

2 Haunted Hotels

Perhaps it's just the sheer volume of visitors they have seen over the years; perhaps all those long-departed guests and drinkers from the distant past leave some trace of themselves in the fabric of such places – but hotels, motels, village inns and public houses undeniably attract more than their fair share of phantoms, apparitions and things that go bump in the night.

A ROOM WITH A SPOOKY VIEW

HOLLINGBOURNE WRAITH

Back in June 2002, I spent a hot few days walking the North Downs Way through Kent. A bare 35 miles (56km) from my destination in Canterbury, I had booked to stay overnight at the grandly named Manor Hotel in Hollingbourne. This place turned out to be a magisterial red brick, early 16th-century house now owned by two very hospitable gentlemen who had retired from the London rat race. They had two or three spare rooms in which they occasionally put up an assortment of ramblers, businessmen and sightseers. Their house is a fantastic rambling edifice full of original features, including some lovely Tudor lead-paned windows.

After a good night's sleep, I was served a full English breakfast at the large oak table in the dining room. To my right was a large open fireplace, the door to the kitchen was over to my left and directly in front of me was a wall with an old door and a row of panelled windows set back into antique frames. I could clearly see beyond into an unlit corridor with a small framed picture and faded wallpaper on the wall beyond. At the left end, the corridor turned at a 90-degree angle to the right, following the contours of the house to another oak door leading, I imagined, to what was once a pantry or storeroom. The right end of the corridor terminated in a set of stairs that led to one of the upper levels. I was on my own in the room and could hear my host bustling about in the adjacent kitchen.

As I was tucking into my breakfast and reading that day's *Guardian*, I looked up and saw an old lady carrying a basket of washing from the assumed "pantry" along the corridor and up the stairs. Her lower half was obscured by the wall, but I saw her top half quite clearly. She was wearing what looked like a black dress, a white apron, and a white bonnet. She was walking reasonably fast and I didn't catch any details of her face, though I presumed she was old by her slightly stooping stature and old-fashioned clothes. I thought nothing of this at the time; after all, it's perfectly normal for a country B&B to employ a maid or cleaner.

After he had finished tidying up, my host joined me at the table for a morning cuppa, and I enjoyed quizzing him about the history of the house. I am a keen history aficionado with an interest in folklore and the paranormal, so it was obvious that our conversation was going to lead on to the spookier parts of the old house's story. While discussing the extensive renovation work they had been doing over the previous two years, I discovered that the wing of the house beyond the wall was unused. They had yet to do any work there and the doors at the end of the corridor were locked. The staircase I mentioned was unstable and was also not used. In any case, it led only to two extra empty bedrooms, both in sore need of repair. In fact, that whole wing was a later 17th-century addition to the house, which at the time was completely closed off. The owners didn't employ a maid or a cleaner, and there were no other guests in the hotel apart from myself.

So who was this old lady I saw? I never mentioned the "maid" to my host but did ask if any of his guests or former owners had ever reported any ghostly goings-on. Sure enough, among certain sporadic unexplained nocturnal noises, there were reported sightings of an old lady in various parts of the house, dressed in a servant's garb of the late 18th/early 19th century. I smiled internally and nearly dropped my sugar lump. With no inexplicable chills, vaguely sensed presence or excited neck hairs, I had, for the first and only time in my life, genuinely seen a "ghost" – either that or my hosts had served me up some extra special mushrooms with my breakfast.

David Wingfield, Nottinghamshire, 2008

HOTEL ROOM APPARITIONS

In October 2002, my wife and I spent three days in an old New York City hotel, about two blocks from Times Square. At about 3:30am on the morning of 27

" *He floated towards me, his features outlined in a faint neon green...* "

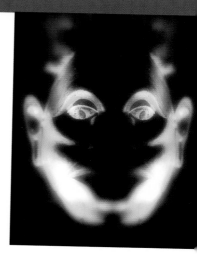

October, I heard my wife awake to go to the bathroom. Once she had returned to bed, I went there myself. I had turned off the bathroom light and was attempting to feel my way to my (left) side of the bed in the darkness, when I noticed a tall, dark figure standing in front of me at a right angle to my body. I was convinced no one had entered the locked room. Suddenly, this figure, perhaps 6ft 2in (1.9m), raised both of its arms and moved toward me as if to embrace or grab me. In a defensive motion, I swatted at it and it disappeared. Immediately, I observed the image of a clean-shaven man, in his 50s or 60s, moving across my line of vision from my left. The image turned to face me, floated toward me, then backed away. His facial features were clearly outlined in a faint neon green. His torso was also visible. Looking at him, I saw that his body appeared to have an oily film moving upon it, very similar to the appearance of soap bubbles blown by a child, when the oily film can be seen in the sunlight before they burst.

Immediately upon seeing this, I also observed a third apparition, darker and not as prominent, moving across my field of vision from my left. It was helmeted, and my impression was that it was an astronaut. Its body seemed rather bulky, but it simply floated around the room with the same 'oily' quality. I wasn't scared, but delighted that I was actually seeing such apparitions. Feeling for furniture, I then realised I was not on the left side of the bed, but on my wife's side to my right. I moved around to the left side and sat on the bed, watching the old man and 'astronaut' continue to float around for perhaps two or three minutes. I also considered that the 'astronaut' might be a fire-fighter with a helmet and oxygen pack. As the old man faced me for several seconds,

I observed a large bright green circle on his right cheek. I did not speak to the apparitions, fearing they would disappear. The room had a murky appearance with a faint green haze. After those few minutes, the figures were no longer visible. Eventually, I drifted off to sleep.

As we ate a late breakfast in the city, I told my wife of the incident. Declaring that I had been neither dreaming nor intoxicated, I had no trouble convincing her. As a precaution, she immediately purchased a cross pendant from a street vendor. Returning to the hotel, I asked the receptionist if anyone else had reported such activity. He replied no, adding that he had only worked there for four months. After hearing my story, he offered us a Bible to place in our room, as we were staying one more night. I placed it on a nightstand, and as I closed the door to rejoin my wife in the lobby, the door made the most mournful creaking sound. Until then, it had not creaked at all, but did so for the rest of our stay.

That night, my wife would not allow me to leave the lights off in the room, though I would have welcomed a second chance to see the apparitions. Given another opportunity, I think I would have spoken to them.
Jared Keeler, by email, 2003

THE DEFOREST MOTEL
Back in the late 1960s my parents bought a motel business, the DeForest Motel, in Susanville, California. We lived in the 'home' part of the motel, which had the lobby/ office in front and our house behind. It had old room units on the right hand side and a line of new units on the left. It was two blocks off the town's main street. That's why we seemed to get customers last, after the Main Street places had filled up. We did have a couple of notable guests stay with us, like the actor Tim Conway, who'd been in the TV show *McHale's Navy*, and one of the *Hawaii Five-O* actors who played Chin Ho on that show. I remember being introduced to both of them in the lobby.

But the motel was haunted. Some of the college guys who rented rooms with us reported strange experiences, like the one in unit 29 who saw a sort of 'spectre' like a white glow or mist in a doorway. My Dad saw 'it' too, in the doorway of the kitchen, as he sat minding the lobby alone one night and watching TV. Sitting in the chair, he felt chills and turned to look behind him – 'it' was hovering in the doorway. He asked 'it' to come and watch TV, if 'it' wanted to. 'It' just went poof and vanished.

Other parts of the motel had a bad feeling. My brother and I tried a bedroom set up in the attic, which you got to by a spooky staircase, but that didn't last long. One night I felt an entity watching us from the doorway, and woke up very scared. On other occasions I thought I glimpsed shadowy figures. We told our parents about how scary it was in the attic, even in the daylight. They moved our bedroom out of there. It was above the lobby, and my feeling was that there was 'something' from the past still there – something very bad. Maybe old man DeForest had done something awful years ago.

The basement was just as bad; I always thought there was possibly something buried down there, under a kind of door or hatch in the floor, over on the dark, left hand side. My parents set up a ping-pong room down there for my brother and I, and we had a frightening encounter while playing. Something was in that dark corner... and something threw a piece of cedar bark and nearly hit my brother in the head.

None of this was good, and one time we even had a visit from a local minister. My dad played him a tape recording of strange sounds he'd made one night. The clergyman was so scared by it he never came back.

After all the odd experiences, my family had a bankruptcy on the motel, and we moved out of the state. But one misfortune after another has been my family's lot since then. And it makes me wonder – why?
Neal Allen, by email, 2010

De Forest Motel
One Block North of Main Street
at the center of
Susanville, California

APPROVED

HAUNTED HOSTELRIES

A PUB FULL OF GHOSTS

I work in a small town pub in King's Lynn, a notoriously haunted town in Norfolk. On weekends I work as the cleaner, before going on to work in the kitchen. There have been several occasions when I've been downstairs on my own (the landlord having gone back upstairs to sleep for another hour or so) and strange things have happened.

The most notable was a few weeks ago. I'd just swept the large wooden floor in the bar area and was heading down towards the restaurant (or carvery) with a dustpan full of the usual pub rubbish. Hearing footsteps, I turned and looked back towards the other end of the pub. The large sweeping brush was still where I had left it, leaning up against the bar. As I watched, the brush jumped and then the footsteps returned, this time running toward me.

Of course, being the total coward that I am, I decided to run quickly away from the area and hid in the carvery until the landlord came down. When I told him of the occurrence, he just gave a shrug and said the same type of thing happened upstairs too. So far, there have been several 'ghosts' both seen and heard: a man in a frilly collar in the kitchen by the head chef, a little girl reaching out for a vase of flowers in the bar by the landlord, a little boy upstairs (supposedly a suicide or murder victim; I forget which) and a large violent man (this is who, it's believed, I had the misfortune of encountering).

I'm not sure what happened... but I'm getting used to things like this in the pub now.

Name withheld, by email, 2004

SHIP INN SPOOKS

When I was a young boy I lived in a large public house called The Ship Inn in Wellington in Somerset. It's one of the oldest buildings in the town, and lots of strange things happened there – so much so that my parents eventually tired of coping with it and moved out.

There are a few memories that linger on now, almost 20 years later. Once, I saw a figure move out of one wall, then glide through another at the end of a long corridor in the living quarters of the pub. It was particularly strange as he looked like a black-and-white image: perfectly clear to see, but having no colour. Customers at the pub would often see a black dog in strange places around the premises, sometimes even within locked rooms. My mother reported items of furniture moving on their own when she was hoovering. Probably the most menacing memory revolves around dad. My father would often have to change the barrels in the cellar for the beer pumps. Once I remember him running up from downstairs, the blood drained from his face, visibly shaken. He wouldn't tell me why he reacted like that, then or now!

I'm still not sure if I believe in a supernatural world – but this makes me think!
Paul Warhurst, by email, 2003

BREAKING GLASS

In 2001, I had not long moved into the White Hart at Wymondham, Norfolk, as a live-in manager. The pub was an old staging post, and what was now a pool room on the side had once been a Masonic Temple. It was quite a strange place to live.

I had organised a friend to collect my belongings from my old flat and bring them to the pub for me. He had picked up my stuff with two other friends and they took it all upstairs, as I had to work behind the bar – having just taken over, I had no other staff. Once all my boxes and furniture had been moved upstairs, the three of them joined me in a few thank-you bottles of Newcastle Brown Ale.

My friends were staying the night, as it was quite a distance home. The pub was big, so all four of us had a room each. It was just gone midnight when I heard the pub doors being shaken. I just thought that whoever it was needn't think that rattling the doors would get them a drink after time when I was about to turn in. At this point, the internal doors started being shaken. I figured it wasn't someone trying to get in but someone trying to get out! I put on my dressing gown and was going to go downstairs when I heard the sound of glass breaking. There was no phone as we were waiting installation. I assumed my friends were asleep and decided to leave whoever it was down there. They wouldn't be able to get out and at least they would be calmer or out cold in the morning when I could deal with it. Eventually, the smashing glass stopped and I fell asleep.

In the morning, I went down nervously, not knowing quite what to expect. There was no glass, no breakages, no open doors, and no people. "It must have been a dream", I thought. One by one my friends awoke. Each of them asked what on earth I had been up to smashing glasses in the early hours!

I looked into some of the history of the building. There had been a fire there 150 years before. A man had been trapped inside and had reportedly tried to

smash his way out of the windows, but they were too small. The doors were all locked. After a little discussion, my friends and I figured that must have been what we had all heard that night.
Lynsey Drewitt, Norwich, 2006

THE GHOSTS OF TRAITOR'S COURT

Around 1985 or 1986, I accepted a position as assistant manager of a restaurant/ bar in the town of Ancaster, Ontario. The place was divided between two floors: the ground floor resembled a roadhouse, the upper floor was supposed to be a fine-dining lounge, which never took off. The kitchen was located on the upper floor, which meant that if someone in the lower level wanted food, the bartender would have to call upstairs using an intercom system.

One Saturday morning, I arrived at 9.45am to open up with two employees, Sheila and Dan. I unlocked the front door and we all went to the bar to have a quick coffee before starting work. As we were sitting there, the intercom system came on as if by itself. This could only mean that someone was using the upstairs intercom. I remember not being able to understand what was being said, but I grabbed both employees and all three of us went upstairs to see who was there. There was no one. We searched the entire place and found no one; and I knew no one had left because I had locked the door behind me when I came in, and it was still locked.

As we stood puzzling over this, the intercom came on again and asked: "Who are you people?" By this time, we were freaking out. Feeling stupid, I asked, "Who are you?" The response that came back in a mournful, shaky voice was, "I'm so cold."

By this time, none of us was in very good shape. We searched every square inch of that building and, again, found no one.

I have since heard that intercom systems like this one are able to pick up CB traffic, police radios, and so on. However, the voice we heard didn't seem to fit in with this, and, moreover, seemed to answer us when we asked a question.

The background of the building is as follows: the bar was named 'Traitor's Court'. The reason for this is that during the War of 1812, the US, upset with the British practice of impressing American sailors, invaded Canada a number of times. These invasion attempts were repulsed through a combination of British leadership, the reputation of Indian savagery in battle, and the ineptitude of certain American generals. However, the British leadership on the spot always worried that the population of Upper Canada (as Ontario was then known) would prove seditious, because so many of them had left the US after the Revolutionary War, either because they were Loyalists or were attracted by cheap land. Consequently, during the summer of 1814, trials known as the Ancaster Assizes were held in this very building. Fifteen people were sentenced to death here, mainly on trumped-up charges. And although the actual executions took place at the British fortifications on Burlington Heights, about five miles away, I firmly believe something stayed in the old courthouse.

Once, on another occasion, I went upstairs to the kitchen to get something, knowing no one was up there. As I got to the top of the stairs, I saw a bus cart roll by itself across the entire length of the dining room. Lights went on and off and items moved by themselves. I never had anything as dramatic as the voice over the intercom happen again. These days, the place is still open under a different name (the Coach & Lantern), and they even advertise that it is haunted!
Anon, FTMB, 2004

3 *UFO Sightings*

Unusual things are seen in the sky the world over on a daily basis, and 'Unidentified Flying Objects' are one of the most widespread of all mysteries. But what are they? Aliens in spaceships? Interdimensional visitors? Balls of plasma, or some other little-understood natural phenomenon? Here, we present sightings of everything from flying triangles and gigantic mother ships to weird 'aliens' and mini-UFOs.

AERIAL ENIGMAS

THE TURKEY THAT SAW UFOS

"The universe is a puzzle beyond reckoning," my dad used to say. He was a pilot and certified airplane engineer. He loved to fly biplanes in barrel rolls and land them with the engine turned off. A daring individual, he served as a plane inspector in WWII. His eyesight was keen without glasses and his sightings of unidentified objects began in the late 1940s. Our home was near a Nike Missile Base in a small, unincorporated village in Michigan surrounded by farms and apple orchards; so perhaps that open countryside had something to do with what he saw.

Dad kept a journal with sketches that I only had a chance to glance through before my brother destroyed it after his death. But whatever dad saw, I know our pet turkey saw it too. She always stretched her neck up straight and gave the warning call for hawks when they were so small they looked like tiny black dots in the sky. This skill of hers was important because my grandfather, who also lived with us, raised white king pigeons, vulnerable to attacks. However, the hawks were not always in her sights. Many times odd flying objects passed overhead. Long before the triangular-shaped flying wings were supposedly sketched on a drawing board, she was spotting them in modified shapes. I know this because my father dated his drawings from the late Forties.

In any event, many objects he spotted in the sky were definitely not flying wings. One day in 1957, around noon, the turkey gave her call when both my dad and grandfather were in the yard, so they looked up. Seven shiny objects were floating above them and seemed to be falling earthward. Dad at first couldn't tell what shape they were until he estimated they had reached approximately 10,000 ft (3,000m): they were perfectly round, reflecting brilliant sunlight, and possibly 30 ft (9m) each in diameter. As they watched, the objects moved into a straight-line formation with a long black cigar-shaped one off to one side as all of them accelerated at an impossible speed leaving no vapour trail.

His story rested in the back of my mind along with another odd tale in which 70 people reported seeing a blimp-like object at dusk floating slowly over the trees near Pontiac, Michigan, in the late Sixties. At least the Pontiac Press newspaper reported that oddball incident. My parents had seen it as well and said it had portholes and looked like a giant-sized hamburger in a bun. But the portholes were even darker than the middle part. They didn't bother to report it because the representative at the Nike Base always denied seeing things on their radar, even when our turkey noticed them. I thought this particular UFO was extra strange because it changed colour from grey to dark shades of pink and orange and only moved at about 10mph (16km\h).

I might as well get another story off my chest. When my husband and I were students at SIU Illinois, we lived in Makanda in an unincorporated, sparsely populated area near the Ordil Munitions Plant (that was also rumoured to be a Nike Base; I never learned whether this was true or false). One night at 11 o'clock we went out to walk our dog and literally bumped into our very conservative neighbours. "Look up!" they said, in excited tones. "We have been out here almost an hour."

Above us a light moved smoothly in a southeasterly direction, and then suddenly it danced wildly, ricocheting across the sky; then it moved north like a normal passenger plane before it made another crazy, zigzagging pattern. We watched it spring across the moonless sky in one direction then another for 15 minutes. Then we walked our dog and returned home, leaving our neighbours still staring at the frenetically zipping bright light. I wondered if we actually saw more than one object since the size of it changed so often.

Years later, when I was visiting friends, I shared the story about the turkey

" They looked up and saw that seven shiny objects were floating above them "

spotting strange flying objects. Their neighbour, who had been a rear tail gunner in a B17 in WWII, told me that he had seen an unidentified round flying object up very close. It had happened in 1957 on a rural road in East Saint Louis when he naively was trying to help his wife have her baby. Frank (name changed), his wife and her mother climbed in their used and battered Chevy and he drove them on a bumpy unpaved road across the river from St. Louis, thinking that would help break the waters and hasten the birth.

As they bumped along on the dark unpaved road, a bright light suddenly showed on the hood of the car. Frank rolled down the window and looked out, thinking it was a helicopter, but to his surprise it made no sound and kept pace with his car.

When it lowered even closer, about 25 ft (7.6m), he could see exact details underneath it because of its bright lights. Three reversed bowls beneath it appeared to be landing pads. And strange hieroglyphs could be seen that fit none of the languages Frank was familiar with through his advanced military training. He and his wife and mother-in-law were very frightened, so he gunned the engine, but the round object, with a diameter he guessed was about the length of a car, kept pace directly in front of them. Then it suddenly accelerated again, emitting no sound or smoke, and disappeared. Seven years later, when his daughter mentioned the incident in school, they were shunned and had to move away from their community. I wondered if there was a Nike Base near East St Louis, but never tried to find out.

Everything seemed fine in Oregon. Dad didn't spot anything here. I never saw any of the wild turkeys around us give a call for a hawk, probably because hawks and turkey vultures are constantly in the skies. I saw nothing odd in the sky until two months ago when I was driving due west of Eugene in broad daylight and an object flew over my car at a rate of speed comparable to a jet. But, oddly, it was rectangular in shape with an extremely shiny silver surface that seemed to undulate, like controlled oscillating ocean waves. It had a thin black bar running the full length beneath it and slightly curved black sides that were about one tenth the width of the shape itself. The top of it melded with the sky as it moved smoothly into the distance directly ahead of me. It made no sound and had no exhaust. I wondered if it could be the invisible cloak that I read our military is experimenting with.

But one thing is certain in my mind: UFOs of various descriptions are real, and they have been seen and documented centuries before our own era.
Ellyn Cummens, Eugene, Oregon, 2010

INVISIBLE TARGET

At 11.30pm on the Saturday night of 18 August I went into my back garden in Surrey to make sure that the gate and garage were closed before I went to bed. My cat was following me around the garden, grabbing at my leg in a playful manner. In my shirt pocket was my pen, which also has a laser pointer in the end. So (keeping the light source away from my pet's eyes) I shone the beam along the grass, darting this way and that for the cat to chase, which he did. He soon got bored with that game and went inside the house.

It occurred to me that I had never thought about how far the laser beam would reach, having only ever used it indoors for highlighting facts and figures during presentations, so I pointed it at a roof of the house that backs on to my own. I was delighted to see the little red dot appear on the tiles. Encouraged by this, I then aimed the laser at a group of trees some distance away and again saw the dot appear in the tops of the trees.

Well, the sky's the limit, they say, so I tried to see if the beam would reach the clouds, which seemed fairly low. Alas, I couldn't see the red dot at all. But just an instant later the dot appeared momentarily, about 50 ft (15m) above my head. It was reflecting off something that was invisible to the naked eye. The beam had bounced off what appeared to be a flat-planed surface. The beam magnifies the slightest hand tremor when used at a distance, and this meant that the beam wobbled, making a smooth flat pattern on the invisible surface.

The whole incident lasted no more than a couple of seconds, as whatever the target had been, it had moved on. I frantically searched the sky with the laser pointer, but didn't have another 'hit'.

I stood for a while looking at the sky trying to work out what had happened. It wasn't pitch black, and there was still some background colour to the sky. So, if it had been a bird, I would have seen it. Also the contact was too long to be a bird in flight, and the target area too large (I estimate that with the beam 'wobbling' I had illuminated over a square metre of the 'invisible' surface). It can't have been an insect – it would be stretching credibility to the limit to think that I had managed to latch onto such a tiny target and keep it within the small pinprick of light, following an unpredictable flight path.

What did I intercept? Whatever this thing was, it was hovering over my house and it was too low for comfort! I live under the flight paths to Heathrow airport, so it is a highly monitored patch of airspace. Maybe this object was flying low to avoid radar detection?

There was no sound – other than a sharp intake of breath from myself – during the encounter, and I saw nothing other than the reflected light from the beam. This target was sitting just above my head and I didn't have the slightest idea that it was there (sometimes you get the feeling that you are being watched, but not on this occasion).

What is a little unnerving is the fact that we have skylight windows at the back of the house, so this thing could have been watching us all evening.
Alan Howard, Walton On Thames, Surrey, 2003

THE MOTHER SHIP

When I was coming home from school one day in 1965 or 1966, accompanied by a handful of compatriots, I saw a gigantic 'mother ship', floating between some clouds. It was several hundred feet long and clearly visible for at least 10 minutes. Strangely, although I stood transfixed by the sight for the entire time, the others (including a cousin and the form captain) walked on as if nothing odd was happening. When I caught up with them at the swings nearby, nobody mentioned it and as far as I know it didn't enter the *Diss Express*, our local Suffolk newspaper.

A few years later, I read *UFOs: Operation Trojan Horse* by John Keel. In it there was mention that this particular UFO had been seen all over the world as well as an illustration of it (a big black needle shape at a 45-degree angle). Later still

I read one of Douglas Adams's sequels to his *Hitch-Hiker's Guide to the Galaxy*, which mentioned The Ashes being stolen from Lords cricket ground under everybody's nose and only the two main protagonists seeing the UFO and occupants that did it: This, Ford Prefect explained to Arthur Dent, was a SEP (Somebody Else's Problem) and that was why it was invisible to them. This made a sort of sense to me and explained the mysterious reaction of my chums – it was none of their business, so why acknowledge its presence?
Tony Sandy, by email, 2011

FLYING TRIANGLES

Back in 1979 I was about 20 years old and working as a stock boy at a department store in Frederick, Maryland (Woolco, since bankrupt). I was out in the parking lot behind the store killing time (a necessary learned behaviour for stock boys) with my co-worker Jeff. There were large truck trailers on the parking lot that were used for the storage of goods that didn't fit in the stockroom inside. We were out there to retrieve something from one of the trailers when I noticed this thing in the sky (I have a habit of scanning the skies). I exclaimed to Jeff to look, and we watched as a black (or darkish) triangle floated in the sky above us, seemingly quite a distance up. It was steady in its position, directly overhead, but then lazily started to circle and ascend until it reached a point at which it was no longer discernable to our eyes. Periodically, Jeff would sneeze – he was one of those people who sneeze when looking up (a little odd in itself, I've always thought)

The whole thing lasted about five minutes, I'd say. At the moment I first saw the triangle, it was about the size of a thumbnail at arms length, and obviously got smaller as it (seemingly) ascended. It gave the impression of being solid and did not change shape. Nor did it glow, but this happened in the middle of a summer's day.

I happened to run into Jeff about six years ago; I hadn't seen him since about 1980. We chatted about the past and what we were doing now, and then he said (without any prompting from me), "Hey, do you remember that time…"

I knew what he was going to say, and we discussed the event again; our memories of what happened were identical. It was nice to have him bring it up, since through the intervening years I had started to wonder whether this had just been a very vivid dream that I had incorporated into my memory as a 'real' event. It was, in fact, a 'real' event after all.
Anon, FTMB, 2002

A strange thing happened to me in York in the summer of 1978, when I was 10 or 11 and in my final year of primary school.

At lunchtime one day, my mate and I were sitting on a bench with a high wall and poplar trees on the other side behind us. For no particular reason we both looked behind us, and there, level with the tops of the trees, was a triangular object, about the size of a camper van. It was orange/red and silver/white – a sort of a raw aluminium colour.

As we watched, frozen, the object suddenly tipped forward and I broke away and ran like hell. I thought my mate had followed, but when I reached the opposite side of the playground I looked back and he was still standing there, looking up, although the object had gone. A sort of heat haze was left in the air. My mate refused to talk about what he had seen, but did acknowledge that he had seen something.

Eventually, we went to secondary school and the event was forgotten until about 15 years later when I bumped into my old friend in town and, in conversation, he suddenly said, "Do you remember when we where in the playground and…?" The story matched my own memories of that day.

I had nightmares about this event well into my 20s. My mother remembers me talking about it, and telling me not to mention it to anyone. Didn't want her son to be classed as nuts, I suppose.

Martin Hunt, York, 2003

UNIDENTIFIED SUBMARINE OBJECT

In 1979, when I was 10 years old, my family spent a holiday at a caravan site in Trimingham near Cromer in Norfolk. My dad took us all fishing off the beach below the cliffs where our caravan site was. It was dusk when my mum took my younger brother back up the steep steps to put him to bed. My sister escorted them, taking our only torch, and was under instructions to return with it. Earlier my dad had been talking about Neptune, god of the seas. We had imagined a great giant with a beard and fork arising up from the sea.

In the eerie twilight, a small black shape emerged out of the water quite some distance away. We watched as it came steadily towards us, wondering what it could be. My dad stood up to get a better look at it. It was large, about the size and shape of an orca whale's fin but thicker. Somehow I knew it wasn't an animal. It didn't move erratically or submerge and emerge again, but came purposefully and silently in a straight line directly towards us out of the gloom.

I realised my dad was quite alarmed. We both instinctively knew that what was out there was 'wrong'. He grabbed the fishing rod and held it up like a weapon, shouting at my sister to turn the light off. She was coming back down the cliff steps bouncing the light around. Immediately the thing advancing towards us stopped about 30 yards (27m) away and stayed there for what seemed like ages. I got the feeling it was observing us as we prepared to run back up the cliff steps should it get any nearer.

Eventually, it moved off horizontally along the water and out of sight into the night. We packed up hastily and retreated back to the caravan in case it should return. The next day, we were travelling home from our holiday. My dad asked an old fisherman if he'd seen anything strange along the coastline. He said that he had but didn't seem to want to elaborate. My dad, sister and I believe that we were either witnesses to an alien spacecraft (under the water) or to a submersible developed by the Ministry of Defence, which has a base in Trimingham.

Tracy Kinsella, Hitchin, Hertfordshire, 2011

LIGHTS OVER COVENTRY

At about 10.15pm on Good Friday (10 April) 2009, I stepped outside my house in Allesley, Coventry, to check that the car was locked up and noticed a moving, illuminated cloud. This hovered in the centre of my vision, moved to the right and split into two, then fused back into one and moved left. My wife and I watched this phenomenon for about 20 minutes. The same sequence was repeated many times. At first we thought it could be a police helicopter, but there was no noise. Our next hypothesis was ball lightning, but there was no rain and no thunder. I'm aware that many UFO sightings report an object splitting in two, but this didn't seem like anything other than a natural event of some sort. It was quite beautiful: an appropriate sight for Good Friday.

Dr Simon Cooke, Coventry, West Midlands, 2011

UFO OVER LOUGH NEAGH?

I was born and have lived most of my life in Northern Ireland. As I was born in the early Eighties, it was a very common sight to see helicopters of various descriptions belonging to the military flying about at various times of the day and night. I therefore knew them by sight very well indeed and because they were so common we rarely took much notice of them. However, the following incident took place about a year after the end of the Troubles, when the security level

" *It hovered in the centre of my vision, moved to the right and split into two* "

had been lowered but the military presence was still maintained.

I was living in a bungalow along the shore of Lough Neagh; the view of the Lough was hidden by a small strip of trees. The area was rural and fairly sparsely populated. One evening when I was about 13, my brother, who was then about six, and I were outside our house in the garden and saw to the north a very bright light moving above the tree line. It drew our attention initially by its brightness, but we quickly realised that it was also moving in a very erratic and bizarre manner.

The light appeared to be perhaps 20 times larger than a star or planet appears in the sky. The light moved up, down and looped about then stopped dead. It then began moving again and resumed its erratic and very quick motion. At times it appeared to move back on itself in very sharp and intricate movements. This occurred about three times, with the object moving very fast towards the east and then stopping dead each time. After the final pause the object began to move again and then shot away to the east extremely quickly and vanished from sight. In all it must have flown about a half mile (800m) above the trees.

I must emphasise that I have never seen a helicopter or plane that could manoeuvre in this highly erratic manner or at such speed. I have often thought about this incident and wondered if it was a military vehicle or weapon being tested on the shoreline above the trees. However, I have never seen any vehicle or weapon which is able to move in this fashion or which gives off such light. I would be very interested to hear of any suggestions as to what I might have seen.

Bronach McElhone, by email, 2010

DISC ATTACKED

This incident occurred sometime in the late 1970s (I don't like being impre-
cise with details, but I was only 10 or 11 at the time, and the only way I can be
roughly sure of the date is that the person I experienced this with was a friend
of mine and we used to spend our spare time together). We were walking up
Sandown High Street on the Isle of Wight. I am pretty sure it was a Sunday afternoon, as everything was closed, and it must have been winter, as there wasn't
a soul around. Our attention was drawn to a sound that I can only describe as
very loud grinding of gears coming from above. It was an overcast day but there
was a break in the clouds and into this break flew a silver disc, the Sun glinting
off it as it passed overhead. This was followed a few seconds later by a Lightning
aircraft (subsequent service in the RAF leaves me pretty certain on this point).
As the Lightning passed through the break in the clouds, a flash was seen from
its port wing and a missile launched, presumably at the disc. My friend and I
ran in the direction that the object and aircraft flew in, but we neither saw nor
heard anything further. I don't recall any mention of this in local media and our
parents were pretty nonplussed when we told them.
David Bruin, by email, 2010

GIANT BUBBLE

A few years ago, my brother-in-law and I set up his telescope to view a lunar
eclipse. The eclipse was in full swing and we had grown bored of looking at it
through the telescope, so he began to try to locate several interesting stars. I
stood in the shadow of the fence just generally looking around at the sky.
Suddenly, something came over us. It was at treetop level, was completely
transparent and fluid, but the lights from the houses and streetlights reflected
off its leading edge, which seemed to change shape like a line of geese flying
over. It wasn't geese; I have been beneath geese and ducks flying over at that
height at night and you can always hear the rush of their wings – this was completely silent. It was like a giant soap bubble, about as big around as a bus, and
it moved very fast. I shouted, and my brother-in-law looked up and saw it before
it had moved out of sight over the other houses in the neighbourhood. We were
both stunned. It was completely beyond our experience.
Anon, FTMB, 2002

AEROPLANE MYSTERY

Recently, my wife Valerie and I noticed a high-flying aeroplane with its usual vapour trail following behind. However, there was also an unusual phenomenon emanating forwards from the front of the plane. It looked to me like a beam of "grey light" being shone ahead by the plane, while Valerie saw it as a kind of grey "tractor beam", as though it were pulling the plane along. The beam, about the same width as the vapour trail, was dead straight like a beam of light; visibility was very clear against a background of blue sky. We watched the plane for about a minute or two until it disappeared into the distance. Despite the many high-flying aircraft we have observed over the decades, neither of us has ever seen anything like this. Can anyone throw any light (pun intended!) on what could have caused this strange phenomenon?
Eric Fitch, Hereford, 2012

TOO CLOSE ENCOUNTERS

BIG AND YELLOW

I am a 54-year-old man. When I was around 11 years old, I was living in a remote part of North Wales and one summer day I was playing with a friend in a field about 50ft (15m) from a small copse. Between 600 and 800 yards (550-730m) away, there were thick woods belonging to the Forestry Commission. We both spotted something moving through the trees about 600 yards away. It was very big and yellow but seemed without any proper shape, probably best described as oval. As soon as we spotted it, we both ran for the small copse behind us, which we had to go through to reach open fields beyond and our homes.

I remember seeing the object and being afraid, after which I have no memory until I came to my senses face down under thick undergrowth in the small copse. I could hear what I can only describe as something breathing through some sort of apparatus like a valve. As I lay there, whatever or whoever it was moved away and the breathing got fainter. Once I could no longer hear it, I jumped up and ran home, but for some reason neither my friend nor I ever spoke to each other about it. Can anyone suggest why I can't remember anything and is there any way I can retrieve the memory? I think about this nearly every day.

Paddy Berry, by email, 2011

RED JUMPER

I am a professional airline pilot, aged 49, and of sound mind.

I was standing on the old Iron Age fort of Old Sarum castle in Wiltshire late in 2011 looking roughly east-north-east at the Old Sarum airfield and Castle Road. As I watched the airfield for activity (there was nothing at all moving) I drifted my gaze along Castle Road where I saw a person in a red jumpsuit, such as a parachutist might wear, drop from the sky into the street, compose himself and walk off towards Salisbury. I had to clear my eyes! There was neither parachute nor the commotion that would have accompanied a parachutist landing in the street. I searched the sky but saw no aeroplane.

I immediately texted my brother to share this event, but he just electronically shrugged his shoulders – he's had his share of such events including time slips.

I know people do not just drop out of the sky into streets, but after a lifetime of being air-minded, I like to think I know what something falling from above looks like! I therefore cannot explain what I "know" I "saw".

David Perry, Stratford sub Castle, Wiltshire, 2012

ORANGE ALIEN

I live in Visalia, California, near South Tipton Street. At about 2pm on 1 November 2010, I saw a cigar-shaped UFO high in the sky. Later on that evening, travelling down 198 into Milo, I saw it again. At some point it appeared to be following me. Then the strangest thing happened. I saw an orange-skinned boy in the middle of the street. He was wearing a blue suit or overalls and had black hair in a crew cut. His eyes were huge and catlike, as if the pupils were in a vertical line. As soon as I saw him, my truck stalled. He stared at me for what seemed like an eternity and my headlights started dimming. I think it was really only about a half a minute. Then he darted away in a Z pattern. He moved so quickly, it was a blur. I saw him at approximately 200 yards near a tree in a matter of seconds.

Russell –, Visalia, California, 2011

MINI-UFOS

SPIDER THING

I was taking an afternoon nap a couple of weeks ago, and was wakened by something floating up around the ceiling. It was the size and shape of a base-ball and was bright red with stringy 'arms', a bit like a spider coming down from the ceiling, though I couldn't see it attached to anything. It was slowly floating down toward me from around the light fixture. It startled me, so I gasped and threw the bed covers off (scaring my two cats in the process). As soon as that happened, it just 'poof' disappeared. I didn't see anything like eyes or discernable facial features, just red stringy things.
Anon, FTMB, 2004

BLUE BAR

In 1994 while staying at my girlfriend's house, I woke in the night and was about to get out of bed to get a drink from the kitchen downstairs.

My girlfriend at the time had a real thing about there having to be as little light as possible entering the room from the windows, so she had a Venetian blind at the window and a pair of heavy curtains covering it too. I can remember being able to discern a light-coloured poster on the wall to my left and the light-coloured pine chest of drawers on my right.

As I was looking around the room, I had to stop and figure out what I was seeing. At the end of the bed was a very faintly glowing blue, bar-shaped light. It wasn't glowing vibrantly, but it was definitely giving off enough light for me to be able to see the pattern of the duvet covering the bed.

Now, I have never seen a ghost and the thought of greys in my room at night strikes the fear of God into me, but this thing didn't scare me. I didn't wake my girlfriend, as I was sure any movement might cause the thing to move or disap-pear. So I just sat and watched.

And after what seemed like ages, it started to shrink over a period of two to three minutes. It was hard to tell it was moving at first, but then I could see it was definitely getting smaller. Then it just disappeared.

Over the years I have returned to the possibility of a shard of light peeking through a gap in the curtains, but the only lights in the street were the orange sodium variety, so I would have assumed that any light would have had a more orange/yellow tinge.

I wish I had tried to photograph it as it's hard to get across the genuine oddity of what I saw.

Dan Roach, by email, 2002

THE TINY LIGHT

One night a few years ago, in my room at my mother's place, I woke up to go to the bathroom. When I got back in my room and closed the door and was just about to get under the covers, I saw a strange light on my desk.

It definitely wasn't the amber power-saving light on my computer monitor, which was switched off. I thought that's what it was before I realised it was moving. I even touched where the monitor light was, because I was still trying to convince myself that it was the little light from the monitor and trying to figure out why it was moving away from the monitor.

It moved at a slow, even pace. I was trying to figure out what it was and got right up close to it: it was about two inches from my face. I still couldn't make out what it was, except that it was light. It moved from left to right about three inches, up about 1/8 of an inch, moved left about an inch or two, moved back down 1/8 of an inch and then disappeared into itself – I mean all the light it was giving off just sucked itself into the centre and it vanished into nowhere.

AK, Toronto, Canada, 2002

WHITE BALLS OF LIGHT

One evening in 2000 I was out in my back garden exercising. It was dark with low clouds in the sky.

Suddenly, out of one cloud a beach-ball-sized white light came shooting down vertically, aiming directly for my head. I ducked very quickly, and it changed direction by 90 degrees and shot over the top of the 6ft (1.8m)-high fence. I looked over the top for any signs of a crater, but there was absolutely nothing. The thing looked like one of those spherical lamps that emanate an electrical lightning effect when you touch the glass. I'm not sure whether it touched me, but I suffered no ill effects nor felt any electrical discharge or heat. It was pure white, unlike a meteorite. I have read subsequently that lights such as these have been seen near crop circles.

Anon, FTMB, 2004

I saw one of these buggers about 14 years ago back home in Wales. It passed between our bungalow and the neighbours' house through a gap in the trees, and was as bright as burning magnesium. For a while I thought it was a very little UFO (which technically, I suppose it was), but then thought it was some kind of lightning bolt. The thing is, it wasn't apparent where it could have actually come from, because if you follow the line between the houses, you just end up crashing straight into a hillside covered in trees about 70 metres away, and there was no evidence of this light dipping and then levelling out – it just appeared, travelling in a straight line, and then disappeared again.

I shall always wonder.
MrSnowman, FTMB, 2004

As a child of about eight or nine, I remember looking through the patio windows on a clear summer evening. The swing in the garden was moving and on it was what I can only describe as a white ball of light, moving in unison with the swing. I immediately ran to the back door where my sister and cousin were sitting on the doorstep. I asked if anyone had just been on the swing; they hadn't. I don't remember going to investigate and simply shrugged the matter off. However, now I wish I had gone to investigate.
Matthew Thorley, by email, 2011

4 *Foreseeing the Future*

Experiences in which people appear to be able to look into the future are surprisingly common, from knowing when an old friend is about to phone to having dreams of events that have not yet taken place. Unlike the abilities claimed by fortune tellers or psychics, though, these seem to be largely involuntary powers, stimulated at times, some of these stories would suggest, by impending disasters...

PRECOGNITIVE DREAMS

SKULL OF ILL OMEN

I am the fourth and youngest daughter of my family. Between my two elder sisters and I came a third daughter, Deborah, who lived for only 10 months before becoming a cot death victim. One day, my mother and I were chatting about the paranormal when she said she was going to tell me something she had never told anyone, even my father. Before I was born, my family lived in an old-fashioned house in Brighton which had a large, coal-fired furnace in the basement. You had to go down and shovel the coal in yourself. My mother explained that she'd always hated carrying out that task, as she found the basement "creepy".

One night, she dreamed that she'd gone down there to put some coal in. When she opened the furnace door, there was a glowing red skull on the coals. She described it as the most horrifying dream she'd ever had and it stayed with her, as she somehow knew it to be a portent that something dreadful was about to happen.

My sister died some days later. Whether or not this dream really was a portent of death, I don't know, but when she told me the story it made all the hairs on the back of my neck stand up!
Anon, FTMB, 2002

DANIEL'S DEATH

Back in the early Eighties, shortly after I entered adolescence, I had a rather strange dream. At junior school I knew a boy named Daniel [surname on file]. We were never particularly close, and our friendship was, at best, an on-and-off affair. He had his chums and I had mine. I lived in Kent at the time, and, as I passed the 11-plus exam and he failed, we went to different senior schools and I rarely saw him.

A year or so after our paths had diverged, I went to bed, promptly fell asleep and started to dream. It was a lovely sunny day and I was sitting on a beach, watching a large number of people playing in the sea. Even though I loved swimming, I felt a tangible dread. Everyone was calling me, beseeching me to come and join them, reassuring me that it was perfectly safe and that there was nothing to worry about. Their cajoling proved effective and I eventually entered the water. Despite my trepidation, nothing happened and I started to relax.

Suddenly, my companions started to panic and desperately tried to get out of the water. I remained, dispassionately observing them as they scrambled onto the beach. Soon I was alone in the sea, a solitary figure standing in the surf, gazing inquisitively at them, wondering why they had so abruptly fled. I was obviously in some danger, as everyone was frantically imploring me to get out of the water, and judging from their gestures, the threat was behind me, out to sea. Strangely, rather than panicking, I calmly started to turn so I could see what had induced such terror in them.

Before I had managed to complete this simple movement, a truly gargantuan wave was upon me, engulfing me before I could even comprehend its enormity, washing me off my feet and submerging me in its darkest depths. I cannot say how long my fragile frame was dragged along by this behemoth, but eventually I was able to struggle to the surface. Looking around, I was shocked to find that the wave had washed the entire world away. I was standing knee-deep in cold grey water, beneath a foreboding, overcast sky. Everything was gone, not only the land and the people, but also sound and colour. Everywhere was uniform and monochrome – a dead place, bereft of life, even time.

I am unsure how long I stood there. I don't think I walked around, but I became aware that someone behind me was calling my name repeatedly, and I turned to see who it was. Daniel was standing there, not too far away but certainly not close. There was a definite distance between us; two separate entities, alone in a desolate place.

I stood watching him. He was imploring me to join him, stating that he was scared to continue on his own. He didn't say where he was going. Even though he was more than familiar to me, I was overwhelmed by complete and utter dread and refused. I am not sure if I actually articulated this, and cannot say definitively that we actually conversed, or how long we stood facing each other: it could have been seconds, minutes or hours. It was at this point that I awoke, terrified and screaming.

I had this dream on the Friday night, and didn't give it much thought once I was awake. My neighbours at the time were racquet sport fanatics, and every week I accompanied them, and their children, Terry (who was a couple of years older than me) and Suzanne (who was two or three years younger than me), to Finsbury Badminton Club. When Terry popped over on the Sunday to tell me they were leaving, he had some sensational news to share. We went to different schools and he assumed, rightly, that I wouldn't be aware of the extraordinary events that had occurred on Friday.

He started by asking me if I knew Daniel. When I said yes, he told me that he was dead. In PE, Daniel had been playing pirates, a popular game that involved the pupils moving around the gym from apparatus to apparatus; if your feet touched the floor, you were out. During the game, Daniel slipped off a piece of gym equipment, fell backwards onto a crash-mat and swallowed his tongue. He was known as a joker, and initially the PE teacher believed he was only pretending to be injured. When Daniel began to turn blue, he realised something was terribly wrong and an ambulance was called. While he waited for it to arrive, the teacher performed mouth-to-mouth resuscitation, which failed to work, although on his way to hospital the ambulance crew had managed to revive him momentarily, but he was dead on arrival at the hospital.

Terry was repeating a story that he had heard after who knows how many retellings and elaborations. I don't believe the teacher initially thought it was a joke, or that Daniel was brought back to life in the ambulance, for the simple reason that the pupils would not have known this had occurred. I have subsequently heard from a mutual friend that he didn't swallow his tongue, but had a hole in the heart, but again this is hearsay and I have no way of finding out the truth. What is significant is that he died on the Friday and that night I dreamt about him. I am sceptical about the paranormal, and I believe that there is a rational explanation for what I experienced. Did I, either consciously or subconsciously, hear someone (probably my parents) discussing what had happened, which then inspired the dream?

Some people may believe that Daniel was afraid to continue his journey after he had died, and was reaching out for someone to help him. Yet, as I previously mentioned, we had never been particularly close, and had rarely seen each other for many months prior to his unfortunate death, so I do not see why he would have contacted me. Of course I may have a particular psychic resonance that he was able to tune into, but if I do it has never bothered me subsequently. Also, as I was alive I don't know what I could have done to help. Maybe if I had followed him I too would have died.

The hall where we played badminton was on a rather desolate stretch of road that ended in an impressively foreboding church, perched atop a crumbling cliff, with a suitably creepy graveyard, and this was where Daniel was laid to rest. Whenever I could slip away from hitting a shuttlecock over a net, I would visit his grave in the hope that it would precipitate another eerie incident, but it never did.

Stephen Watt, Hartlepool, Cleveland, 2012

WHEN DREAMS COME TRUE

I believe that dreaming about things that come true – or occasionally almost true – at a later date is not uncommon. I have had the experience many times. Two recent ones come to mind. The first was when I dreamed that I was with my wife in a long, low building in the company of several small people. The dream occurred between six and seven in the morning. A few hours later, at about 11am, we were in Rhos on Sea in North Wales when a small, elderly gentleman who was standing against a lamp post asked, very politely, if we would care to join his friends in the chapel over the road for coffee and biscuits. We did – and it was a long, low building and all the very nice people inside were small and elderly.

More recently and rather more intriguingly, I dreamed that I was with my wife in the lounge and the time was about 4pm. The doorbell rang and when I answered it there was a polite young man wearing a jacket and collar and tie. He was very apologetic, said he was very sorry but he was in need of a toilet. The next 'clip' in the dream was that my wife and I were standing with our backs to the fireplace when he walked past us – without being directed – to the toilet in the back lobby. I remarked to my wife, "Seems to know the way." A few minutes later, he said thanks and left.

The following day, again we were both in the lounge in the afternoon, this time not dreaming, the doorbell went and the young girl from next door said she was very sorry to bother us but she was just home from school and did not have her house key and needed the loo. She walked straight through the lounge to the toilet; of course she knew where it was, as she lived in a similar house; so, like the man in the dream, she did not need to be told where to find it.

The rather startling bit was a couple of weeks later. Same time in the afternoon, and again not a dream. The doorbell went. Polite young man on the doorstep wearing an identification badge and carrying one of those electronic gadgets that meter readers use. Said he was very sorry, he had just read the electric meter, but needed to use the toilet. This one had to be shown the way.

I try hard to figure out how it works. I seem to remember reading in St Augustine's *Confessions*, the good saint asking God how it is we can see in the future something that has not yet happened. If he was baffled, who am I to complain? My best guess is that our lives are happening in a slightly different way in another dimension, just a short time before they happen here. Anyone got a better idea?

Doug Hall, Knaresborough, North Yorkshire, 2010

PRECOGNITIVE TRIVIA

Like Doug Hall, I have precognitive dreams, but mostly concerning extremely mundane things. For instance, I woke one morning bemoaning the fact I had dreamt about work most of the night. About two months later, I went into a meeting and when a colleague I didn't know came in, I got a feeling of déjà vu. I found I knew what was going to happen and be said for large portions of the meeting. I unnerved one of the speakers when I mimed quite a few of their sentences as they spoke.

I seem to have these dreams four or five times a year. The strangest was about a rod about 8in (20cm) or so that went across in front of me about 3ft (90cm) away. It went from left to right at head level and seemed to oscillate up and down very quickly. Several months later, I had a detached retina in my left eye. While it was being operated on in hospital, I couldn't see out of the eye; but suddenly in my left eye vision I saw what I would describe as a rod oscillating up and down, going from left to right. I think it was a tool that was being used on my eye.

Of course, if we take on board the argument proposed by some astrophysicists

that all time exists at once, precognition doesn't really exist.
Philip Hemmise, by email, 2011

JAMES WOODS IS UPSET

I had a dream that I encountered James Woods the actor. He was dressed in a suit that dated back to the 1960s (which I don't think was significant for this dream, but it was just how I may have seen him in the past from some movie).

This was the most unlikely person I could have been dreaming about. He was not on my mind and I hadn't seen a movie of his lately, so I knew it meant something significant.

He was crying and I could feel the intensity of his pain and anguish. It was so pronounced that the feeling stayed with me for at least two weeks – I just couldn't shake it. In the dream, I consoled him and told him I loved him and that it would be OK, and that I had the deepest concern for him and what he was going through. It prompted me to try and look him up to tell him about this dream, via a website or agent's email, but to no avail.

About two and a half weeks later I saw the news that his brother had died and read an article that said he was visibly upset. I knew then that my dream had been a message. It was crazy to have that feeling of despair stay with me for that length of time and just as crazy that I had been dreaming about James Woods. I just wished there was some way for me to have known what the dream meant and to have warned him.
Bernice Policastro, FTMB, 2006

PRACTICAL DREAMS

There is an aspect of dreaming which seems not to have attracted much attention – that of solving problems – to the extent of revealing 'unknown unknowns'. In my schooldays in the 1930s (I am now 86), my friends and I were much taken by two propositions – first, that the red shift observable in the spectra of distant galaxies might be due to light losing energy and velocity in its passage to us; and second Dunne's concept of serial time. So we began to devise instruments capable of measuring the speed of light, and also recording dreams as Dunne suggested.

After several months we gave up both – nothing remotely like Dunne's experience had occurred, but I had a particular dream which put paid to the velocity of light project. Simply, I dreamed I had a large telescope to which I had added one of our devices (based on a television scanning mirror drum – yielding an image which moved laterally according to speed, it probably would have worked). In my dream, I had used the system, and was writing up the result. In my apparatus, no change in velocity could be found. The key words were "in my apparatus" – what I had measured was the velocity in my kit, not as desired in the space between the nebula and my telescope – a salutary lesson.

Since that first time, I have had numerous dreams that solved problems, most of them not in my mind when I fell asleep. However, there is a radical difference between my useful dreams and the rest – I can recall the former in great detail, while the "normal" fantasy shifts shape and vanishes as I try to recount it.

How does this compare with other people's experience?

Colin Reid, Swindon, Wiltshire, 2011

PREMONITIONS OF DISASTER

9/11 FORESEEN?

It was a morning near the end of summer 2001. I was making my regular drive to work when suddenly a wave of sorrow came over me. Compared to many people in the world, I have a lot to be thankful for, but for a few minutes, all my little problems came to the forefront of my consciousness, and I felt very sad. I even shed a tear or two.

This was very unlike me. I'm usually a stable, stoical, unemotional kind of person; so at the same time I was feeling this sorrow, I was asking myself, "What's wrong? What's wrong? Why am I so sad this morning?" Was it something I'd eaten for breakfast? I was quite puzzled, but after 15 or 20 minutes I shook it off, arrived at work, and forgot all about it…

Until later that day when, at around 4 or 5 or so in the afternoon, a co-worker received a phone call from his wife. After speaking with her for a moment, he turned to the rest of us to say that she had seen on television that the US was under attack, that the Pentagon had been hit and one of the World Trade Center towers had collapsed and the other one was burning.

I live in the Middle East, but I grew up in the New York area and spent most

of my life there. I think my inexplicable sorrow might have been a vague premonition of the sad events of that day.
Jay Gourd, Israel, 2003

It was three days before 11 September 2001 and it was around two am. I heard an explosion far away being carried by the wind. I thought little of that on its own, but then I heard another and another. Then I heard planes coming from the same direction. I genuinely thought that we were being bombed – perhaps by Saddam Hussein – and I ran upstairs and woke my wife. I told her something terrible was happening and that I feared for everybody. I think I just babbled in absolute terror. She got up, made coffee and then came and listened and heard nothing except the planes flying over. I was ready for Scotland's destruction and she went back to bed. Needless to say nothing happened... until three days later!
    I don't really think this was a premonition, because the sounds were real. But my terror three days later was intensified because of it.
Name withheld, by email, 2002

THE 9/11 BIRD
On the morning of 11 September 2001, I was driving a van past a lough in Northern Ireland. It was a section of road that had a low wall by it. To my utter amazement I saw a huge eagle-like bird sitting on a haystack. Honestly, this thing was enormous, with its black wings spread out. I couldn't stop, due to traffic behind me. I did have my camera and now regret not taking a picture. It was only when I got north of Belfast that I learned about the terrorist attack on New York from a tea stall owner. It was months before I realised that the time I saw the huge bird roughly coincided with the attack. Could it have been some kind of symbolic psychic projection, perhaps the Thunderbird that Native Americans used to see or the iconic eagle used as a US national symbol? The RSPB told me it was a sea eagle, but it was much too big for that; it had the wingspan of a small plane or glider.
David Jones, Bangor, Gwynedd, 2011

BRIDGE PREMONITION
I have had a tragic event appear in my dream in real time – that is, when the real event was actually happening. My guess is that this probably happens more often than we're aware of. My dream was about something entirely different, but then

" My sorrow might have been a premonition of the sad events of that day "

in the middle of it I found myself talking to someone about something or other. Suddenly, we were interrupted by a big noise up in the sky. I looked up and cars, trucks, and a bus were falling out of the sky and crashing into the streets around us.

Later, when I awoke, I turned on the TV to see a news report about a bridge collapse in Oklahoma. Many people had driven their vehicles off the middle span of the bridge before realising it had partially collapsed. Many had died. My family is from the area, both the American Indian and European branches. Although I've lost contact with them, I know I still have many relatives there. Perhaps this is why this event entered my consciousness. I don't know – but I don't believe it was a coincidence.

Susan Harmon, FTMB, 2002

GLIMPSES OF THE FUTURE

THE DEVIL'S MUSIC

Around Christmas in 1981 (I think it was), when I was about 25, I saw a televised production of a Stravinsky ballet. I liked the music a lot, and wanted a recording. I thought the piece was called 'The Soldier and the Devil'. I went looking for it in the record stores of the small West Midlands town of Dudley where I was living, but couldn't find it, so I asked if there was a recording available. After a huge ledger was consulted, I was told there was no recording available, so I gave up looking.

About six months later, I had run some errands in town, and was on my way to the bus stop. As I passed a large department store, which I hardly ever went into, the thought came into my head, out of nowhere and very clearly: "If you go into this store now, you'll find a record of Stravinsky's 'Soldier and the Devil'". I recalled that I'd been told it was not available; I was in a hurry to catch the bus, and not in the mood for wild goose chases. But as I continued to walk past the store, the thought nagged away at me with increasing urgency. Go in now! Now! I hesitated, thought about taking a quick look, but then decided I was just being silly. Much better to catch the bus. I then found that I was unable to move. It was as if something was holding me in place, pressing down on my shoulders. I literally couldn't take a step. The only way I could break this paralysis was to go into the store. There was a long fixture of classical records. I started at one end and worked my way through them, cursing myself for my idiocy in missing my bus. In the last section of the fixture I found a cheap Stravinsky recording, made in Czechoslovakia, and called 'L'Histoire du Soldat'. The English notes on the back made it clear that this was my 'Soldier and the Devil'. It cost about £3, and I bought it.

This incident is trivial, but after 20 years I vividly remember the sense of urgency, and the strange and rather frightening feeling of being unable to move from the spot until I gave into this impulse to look at the records. If I ever get a similar compulsion telling me not to get on a plane, I shall certainly listen to it!
Susan Price, by email, 2002

STEVE'S COMING!

In around 1995, I was sitting in a Chemistry lesson at school. I suddenly started saying to the person sitting next to me, "Steve's coming to see us." I would repeat this every so often. Eventually, the lad next to me got cross and told me to stop being silly and shut up.

Anyway, later on, a young adult entered our lesson. Our teacher introduced him as Stephen, a former pupil. I swear I had no idea that this guy was going to show up. I don't even know why I said that Steve was coming to see us.
If it was just a coincidence, then it was a very odd one. Why would I choose the name Steve? Why would I only say it in the very lesson in which Steve actually did come to see us, the fourth of the day?

The great thing was that my fellow pupil no longer had any grounds for saying that I was being silly. I actually felt quite proud of myself!
Anon, FTMB, 2004

PERFECT GOAL

I recently played in a veterans' football tournament in Bangkok, Thailand, and (very unusually) managed to score a spectacular picture-book goal. This was unusual, not only because I am usually utterly inept given a scoring opportunity, but also because I had visualised the goal some half an hour before the start of the game.

This wishful thinking (for that is what I took it for) had me executing a perfect scissor-kick in mid-air past a flailing goalkeeper as the ball dropped from a clear blue sky. Therefore, when this scenario actually occurred, and the ball kicked up off their keeper and was indeed dropping out of a clear blue sky, I simply clicked into autopilot, launched myself into the air and crashed the ball home on the volley, just as I had rehearsed mentally prior to the game.

It is important to note how out of character this is for me as a player. I just don't do that kind of thing and the level of assuredness and lack of panic almost seemed to come from an external source. This is what has got me wondering about the origin of the moment. I knew exactly what to do; there was no question in my mind, no hesitation.

Could this be an example of precognition or simply the power of positive thought, making my wishes and reality converge? Before it happened, I had been pondering the veracity of such events after reading about them in recent editions of *FT*, for example the dream experiments at Maimonides Medical Centre, New York. Was the Universe answering my questions and showing me that in fact these things are real?
Duncan Kaiser, by email, 2011

ADVANCE WARNINGS

DON'T CATCH THE BUS!

Many years ago, when I was living in Kenya, there was a bus drivers' strike.

On the morning in question, I started walking to work, a distance of about two miles. Soon after I passed my usual bus stop, I saw that some buses were actually running. The next bus stop was on a hill, after which the path on that side of the road ended. As I approached the bus stop, a little voice told me not to use it. Stupid as it may seem, I crossed the road, prepared to walk the rest of the way to work, rather than wait at the stop. Within seconds of me crossing the road and continuing to walk down the hill, a car smashed into the bus stop where I would have been standing. Not only did the path stop there, but the fences of the adjoining properties meant there was no way out from the bus stop apart from the approaching path or running onto the road. I was now standing across the road, in shock, looking at the place where I would have been killed or seriously injured.

When I did get to work, happy just to be alive, my bosses were moaning about me being late…

Anon, FTMB, 2004

STORM WARNING

My wife of a little over a year, 'J', tends to have dreams that come true in some form or other, usually within in a day or two. These usually involve everyday family matters, arguments, meetings or other relations. But not long ago, her premonitions manifested themselves within minutes of an occurrence and much closer to home.

We were driving to the mall one afternoon. The sky was a little overcast, the weather slightly drizzly. As we got closer to the mall, the weather got worse. A little windier, a little rainier, but nothing I couldn't handle. As we sat at a red light, my wife interrupted our conversation, saying "I have a bad feeling – please be really careful." I said that, of course, I would, but she was insistent: "No, really, please just be very careful, more than normal".

The light turned green and it began to rain so heavily that we could barely see, even with wipers at full speed. The sky wasn't even that dark, and yet all I could see were taillights and the grey of the water. The cars ahead of us sped up and disappeared from sight, all but one directly ahead of us. I had a chance to change into the right lane and pass it, but after my wife's warning, I didn't even risk that. Instead, I stayed about a car's length behind this car, and used him as my guide.

The wind picked up in ferocity, and we heard snapping; we realised we were trapped on this road lined with huge old oaks leaning over it! Suddenly, a huge

branch fell directly in front of the car in front of me – so suddenly that the driver had no time to stop, and ran it into it, getting caught underneath. The raw, thick base of the branch was in the right lane – exactly where we would have been if I had been driving at my normal speed and had attempted to pass him. I know this because I was mentally battling the desire to do so the entire time. I could only imagine what would have happened if our windshield had been under the fallen timber. Well, my wife was scared shitless; more, I think, from her gut feeling having merit than the actual fright of the event.
Traffic was now at a standstill behind us. The car in front seemed OK and was backing up a little, while the right lane was blocked by the branch. The sound of further tree limbs snapping was all around us.

We pulled into the closest, safest parking lot, branches of all sorts still flying by, and waited for about half an hour until this sudden squall stopped, just as suddenly as it had begun. My wife was still in full panic; I, for some reason, was quite jovial – happy to be alive, and glad I had been given a warning.
Anon, FTMB, 2004

EXPLOSION FORESEEN

I had a precognitive experience last week – even though I don't really believe in them. I was driving home on I-80, and just as I was about one car length behind this car in the slow lane, passing them, it flashed into my mind: "That car's going to blow up." By the time the front of my car was even with the back doors of the other one, the thing did burst into a fireball under the chassis – I mean that f****r exploded! Flames were shooting out from under the whole undercarriage. "F**k," said I, and pulled off onto the shoulder 100 yards further along.

There were three Filipino girls, very shaken up. I didn't know exactly where we were (about 1/2 mile west of the 370 exit, as it turned out) so while I was in my car, fumbling around with the useless highway map, a State Trooper pulled up behind the burning car. I watched a bit. He got them to move farther away from the car and was handling the situation, so I left.

It was very weird that I knew two seconds ahead of time that the car was going to blow. I think there was something that I didn't consciously register, that warned me – a spark, a sub-sonic concussion, something. But if there was, I'm still not aware of it.
Anon, FTMB, 2002

The Odd Outdoors

Strange things can happen out in the countryside: well-known surroundings can become suddenly unfamiliar and walkers can become hopelessly lost; a normal camping trip can become a night of terror; visits to prehistoric sites can unleash strange energies; and even in an urban setting, a straightorward car journey or a simple walk can take a turn for the unexpected... and the unexplained.

LOST

THE CLEARING

It was around June 2001 when my partner and I decided to go for a walk to a favourite spot in the middle of a forest close to Llanbradach Mountain, Caerphilly, near where we lived at the time. We used to visit this particular spot regularly when we were supposed to be in school, but hadn't been up there for around five years. We found it quickly, as we knew the route so well.

The location in question is a clearing in the woods, which forms an almost perfect circle. It always had an untouched feeling, as if we were the only people who knew about it. But on this occasion it was filled with empty beer cans. One of the trees surrounding the area had had a fire lit against its trunk and others had had nails driven into them. In the centre of the circle a collection of sheep skulls had been placed and set fire to. More sheep skulls had been placed on poles scattered around the clearing. As both myself and my partner are pagans we were saddened by this display, probably the work of teenagers who'd found somewhere they wouldn't get caught drinking and had set up the skulls to scare other people away from the area. We spent some time tidying up and buried the skulls in the forest. When we had returned the clearing to something close to its usual state, we decided to lay a blessing on the site, casting a circle and asking for protection over it. When we had finished we returned the same way that we'd come. Not long after this we moved away from the area because my work called for me to be transferred some 50 miles (80km) away.

About nine months later we were visiting Caerphilly and decided to make a trek back to our favourite spot. We entered the woods at the same place we always did and started following our usual route, but after about 20 minutes we were in an unfamiliar part of the forest. On deciding that we must have passed the clearing, we retraced our steps and returned to the original point where we had entered the forest. We were starting to feel a bit freaked out by this, as we had always been able to find the clearing without any problems. We decided to go back into the forest and to conduct a more thorough search for our site. After a very Blair Witch style couple of hours spent getting thoroughly lost in an area that we'd always known so well, it started to get dark. This normally wouldn't have worried us – we'd been through the forest many times at night and normally didn't even need a torch to find our way around. But this time we both got the feeling that we were intruding somehow, and that a presence didn't want us to be there. We decided to get out as quickly as we could, and picked a straight direction to walk in.

For some unknown reason I felt an urge to try to justify our being there and, stupid as it sounds, placed a hand on a tree and said aloud that we meant no harm. Immediately, the uncomfortable feeling lifted, and upon looking round the familiar clearing was visible about 20 yards (18m) down the path behind us. On entering the clearing we saw that it looked completely untouched since the last time we had been there. We stayed for about 10 minutes, still a bit freaked out, and when we had regained our composure, headed home. We have now moved back to the area and visit the site as often as possible. Since then, we've had no further trouble finding the clearing, and have never felt that Pan-like presence again.

Neil –, Caerphilly, 2004

DIZZY DAY AT MARCH HARE LAKE

One day in 2004, I was out walking in Algonquin Park, Ontario, Canada, with my partner (who for the sake of her privacy, I shall call 'Lisa'). We were walking the Mizzy Lake Trail, a seven-mile (11km) walk through forest and wetlands which is designed to bring you in proximity to some of the local wildlife. These shorter trails in Algonquin are easy to follow; every few metres there is a blue disc nailed to a tree to show you the way and keep you to the path. About halfway along we had a bit of a disagreement (basically I called her wimpy because she was moaning about having to walk across bits of wood to get across boggy ground and her balance wasn't very good, and so on) so we ended up walking separately with me in front. Every now and then I stopped to make sure she was close behind me.

As we approached a section at the north-east corner of one of the small lakes on the trail (March Hare Lake) I stopped to check behind me again. There she was, about 30-50ft (9-15m) behind me on the path. I turned around and carried on, stopping after a few more steps at a bend to wait for her. Suddenly I heard a weird noise – like a creaky groan – from the direction I had last seen her in. When she didn't appear on the path I re-traced my steps, thinking that perhaps the noise was some animal coming through the trees that she'd stopped to look at. But she wasn't there. She should have been easy to spot, wearing a bright white T-shirt and light coloured trousers but I couldn't see her anywhere.

"Lisa?" I said, "Where are you?"

There was no reply. I tried again, a little louder this time.

Thinking she was probably hiding to teach me a lesson for going on in front I started to get a bit agitated. "LISA!" I shouted, "IF YOU'RE HIDING YOU CAN COME OUT NOW!"

Still no response – nothing but the sound of a few birds and the creaking of a tree in the light breeze. I started to panic and began yelling her name at the top of my voice, so loudly that I could hear the echo across the lake. But there was still no answer.

I was upset. What if she'd been attacked by a bear or worse and not had a chance to scream or yell for help. Panicking, I frantically ran backwards and forwards for a couple minutes along the path, literally screaming her name and yelling for help, but all was completely in vain. I was resigned to having to call 911 and look for a body. It was a horrible, horrible feeling. Just then the cellphone I had in my backpack gave up the ghost, leaving me with no option but to run to the highway, three miles (5km) away, and call from a payphone at the car park.

So, off I ran, falling over tree-roots and through streams. After about a mile I started shouting her name again and from some way in the distance I heard a response. Not sure whether or not it was her, I carried on running and shouting until I could ascertain that it was. I shouted to stay put and, when I turned a corner and she was standing there in front of me, I fell on her with tears in my eyes.

"Where have you been?" she asked.

And this is where it gets weird.

She had stuck to the path as well, but hadn't passed me. In fact, she was convinced that I was still way ahead and was angry with me for not waiting for her. She had not heard me shouting until I had almost caught up with her, despite my screaming at the top of my lungs. How had she got so far ahead in such a short space of time? We discussed the routes we had walked, and they were identical – basically, along the edge of the lake. There were no short cuts and I'd had to run to catch her up. If she had passed me where I had stood waiting for her at the bend, even given the time I was shouting to her, I would have caught her up sooner. She doesn't walk particularly fast and, given my panicky state, I was moving pretty quickly. So what had happened?

It was very freaky and we've discussed a lot of possible explanations. Lisa was initially convinced that she must have passed me and we just didn't see each other. But there was no way this could be: the path was too narrow, neither of us could have strayed off it, we were both wearing clothes that would have made us noticeable to one another and I was shouting at the top of my voice.

Even if we had somehow missed one another, she couldn't have got as far ahead as she did in the time involved. I mentioned to her the sound I heard, and she said she too had heard a weird noise, but had just carried on walking, thinking nothing of it. It seems to me that the noise may have been linked somehow – it corresponded with the time she 'overtook' me

I've scoured the Internet for any other weird events connected with the area, but nothing has turned up. One thing I have noticed, though, is the name of a couple of the small lakes in the vicinity: March Hare Lake (where the initial event occurred) and Dizzy Lake. It would be interesting to know why they were so named!

Lee Stansfield, Alliston, Ontario, Camada, 2004

SUDDENLY UNFAMILIAR

On the evening of 1 March 2010, I paid a visit to some friends in their new home in the Broadstone neighbourhood of Poole in Dorset. I said goodbye to my wife and left home (in the Parkstone neighbourhood of Poole) at 7.40pm. The journey only took me 15 minutes, as the traffic was light.

After a good evening of chat, during which I drank no alcohol, I set off for home at 11.25pm, having texted my wife to say I was on my way. I drove home the same way I had come – around the large roundabout at Broadstone, down the Lower Blandford Road to Darby's Corner Roundabout, where I took the second exit into the Canford Heath Estate until I came to the mini roundabout, where I took the second exit, which is straight on. Checking my mirror, I noticed a car straight behind me. Within half a mile I should have reached the next roundabout, as there are no more turnings before this.

I had only gone a few seconds down the road when the car started to lean to one side as if I had developed a puncture, the engine spluttered and the car behind me disappeared. It couldn't have turned off because there were no turnings. I found myself driving down a very dark lane with high hedges, but no houses or streetlights. The car was now working perfectly. I didn't know where I was and was quite scared. I pulled over where the road seemed a bit wider and tried to phone home, but my mobile wasn't working. I drove on down the lane for what seemed like miles. Then I came to a T-junction with an old wooden signpost that pointed to the left saying Wimbourne. I thought Wimbourne should have been to my right, but I turned left anyway and within 30 seconds I was amazed to find myself back at the Broadstone roundabout near the start of my journey. I then took the same route again, going past the place where everything had become unfamiliar and arrived home at 11 minutes past midnight, half an hour later than I should have done. My wife asked why I had taken so long, but I was unable to say.

John B Collins, Poole, Dorset, 2010

STRANGE TRIPS

AVEBURY BUZZ

I live about 15 miles (24km) from Silbury Hill and Avebury, and as I enjoy mooching around old places I regularly walk in the area. I had a couple of weird experiences at the Kennet Avenue of standing stones. Once I was showing a friend the avenue; at the point where the road cuts across the avenue, the car radio lost reception but regained it as soon as we got to the other side. And while walking along the inside of the avenue, I got to a point where I felt a buzzing running through my body. I stood there for a couple of moments and carried on walking,

when the feeling left me. When I went back to the same spot, the buzzing feeling started again.
Lloyd Robson, Wiltshire, 2008

MAZE ACHE

The letter from Lloyd Robson stating he felt a buzzing sensation when he walked along the Kennet Avenue of standing stones reminded me of an incident that happened to me many years ago on a trip to Cornwall. I had visited St Nectans Glen near Tintagel and decided to walk to Rocky Valley to see the maze carvings, otherwise known as the Rocky Valley labyrinth petroglyphs. Like many people, I traced the outlines of the mazes with a finger and then I placed my hands on them, palm down, left hand on left carving and right hand on the right one. I instantly felt an ache at the base of my skull. It wasn't disabling, but I knew it was there! I removed one hand and it stopped. I put my hand on the carving again and it began again. I was on my own and decided not to continue with this experiment and I haven't been back since. One day I will and I'll let you know how I get on.
Sally Thomas, Redruth, Cornwall, 2008

STONE CIRCLE SHOCK

I visited the 12 Apostles stone circle on Ilkley Moor, Yorkshire, about 10 years ago on a cold, wet, wintry day. I walked around the circle examining the stones and got what I can only describe as an electric/static shock on touching one of them. Nothing too serious, but enough to cause me to snatch my hand away.
Ian Langdon, by email, 2004

FEELING FLOATY

On 27 May 2008, I was walking along Princess Road in Chelmsford, Essex, from the Army and Navy roundabout towards the Miami roundabout at about 3.30 in the morning. I felt as if I were walking into a wave in the sea and being lifted, although my feet didn't leave the ground. My body became lighter and I felt younger with no aches and pains. I was 39, but I felt 17. This happened twice more at two more places on my walk. To ensure it wasn't just me having a bit of a post-pub funny one, I walked back out of it and into it again and each time I got the same feeling. That night there had been a problem at two power stations including Sizewell B in Suffolk, so there was a lot of power being switched around

> *I put my hand on the carving and felt an ache at the base of my skull*

the country, and I guess there are underground power lines. However, I haven't been able to find any other reports of such a sensation, which was very noticeable and pleasant; in fact if I could repeat it I would! Is any reader aware of such things being reported before?

Dan Smith, by email, 2010

STORMY NIGHT ON BUTE

During the summer of 2010, I went on a cycling trip for a few days to the Island of Bute and Argyll. My mates couldn't get off work on the Thursday or Friday, so I arranged to meet up with them nearer Dunoon on the Saturday. I set off in glorious weather and decided to camp near Colintraive, just a short ferry hop across to the mainland from the north of Bute. I had camped there before and knew a great spot from where I could go and do some canyoning up the burn (stream). This site was ideal, with trees and rhododendrons providing a thick canopy and plenty of dead wood for the fire. It was high up a steep hill from the village and there was a ruined building with just a gable and low walls remaining. An iron fence enclosed the copse and the ground was largely bare earth due to the dark canopy of leaves. The weather in the evening took a turn for the worse and a huge gale blew up. Despite this I managed to get a roaring fire going and thought that my day's labours would ensure a sound sleep. How wrong I was.

I must have decided to turn in just after midnight and I peed on the fire to extinguish it, poured the contents of my kettle on it, then got my shovel and buried it to make doubly sure. To my delight, my new one-man tent was watertight and wind-proof, but the noise of the trees in this mounting storm was almost deafening so sleep was impossible. I put on my radio but, because of my location, was only able to receive Radio 2, and that night they seemed to be having a Kenny Rogers-a-thon. I switched it off because listening to the storm seemed more attractive. Leaves and twigs were now hitting the tent quite regularly and I began to question my choice of pitch in case a larger branch decided to come calling. It must have been around 3.30am when I was thinking that I wasn't going to get any sleep and I opened my eyes. To my puzzlement it looked as if the Sun had risen because the tent was bathed in that kind of light. I was able to see round the tent quite clearly and was a bit confused. After about five seconds it went suddenly pitch black again and I froze. The first thing I thought was that there was someone shining a light, but I could only hear the storm. There had been no lightning or thunder, and the duration of this light had been far too long for a lightning flash anyway.

My imagination then started to run riot; was there someone or something there? But if that was the case why was the light omni-directional? I was seriously bricking myself now and tried to rationalise it as best I could. The nearest dwellings were far down the hillside and I discounted far-off car headlamps shining though the bushes, so my conclusions were now lurching towards the paranormal. I noticed that my snug tent was similar in shape to a coffin! I began to think that perhaps the fence-enclosed copse had been a graveyard and that the ruin was a chapel. For the rest of that fretful night, my tent was pelted with leaves and twigs, as the wind and rain were relentless. When eventually the Sun did rise I managed to relax a bit and dozed lightly, but I decided to get an early exit out of there. At about 7am, I got up and when I opened the tent, the fire was going! Not as big but it was definitely burning despite my efforts to extinguish it.

I made a cuppa and packed up, put out the fire for a second time and donned my waterproofs. By 9am the weather was glorious again and I had to unpeel all my soggy layers. Seventeen miles (27km) later, I met up with my mates who just ribbed me about my experience, with questions about aliens and rectal probes. I could laugh about it then but a few hours earlier I had been as terrified as I've ever been. The best explanation that I have subsequently come up with is that perhaps a fireball might have passed overhead and bathed the area in dim light. There were a few reports that summer of such occurrences, and a friend had seen one near Prestwick one morning and it was reported on the BBC website. As for the fire, perhaps embers deep inside a thick log survived and were stoked into life again by the wind. I would go back – but maybe not alone.
Colin Irons, by email, 2011

6 *Unusual Abilities*

Some people stop clocks whenever they walk into a room, or interefere with televisions and cause computers to crash. Others appear to possess an ability to transport from one spot to another almost instantaneously in a way that would make Mr Scott from *Star Trek* proud. Other unusual powers appear to be of a mental rather than physical variety – but can such weird abilities be real, or are they 'all in the mind'?

ANOMALOUS ENERGIES

FORTUNE FISH

Last week our friend Adrienne's mother sent her one of those cheap fortune telling fish made of red plastic that wriggle around in your hand. As we all sat round her house, she broke it out and we started to play with it. The Chinese translation on the plastic sleeve it comes in basically says each movement of the fish represents something like you being romantic, in love, fickle, false and a few other feelings (surely this makes it more of a mood or personality fish than a fortune telling fish – but I digress).

Adrienne had a go, and we were enchanted by the fish-like movement of the wiggling tail. My wife did it, and it curled up and flipped. Each of them got only one response from the fish, but when I tried it did everything on the list, as well as things I don't think it was meant to do.

It flipped and flopped numerous times, stuck out its tail and wiggled, rolled back and forth, wiggled its head, rolled halfway up my wrist and back into my palm. It even sat up on its nearly two-dimensional (paper thin) bottom edge and made swimming movements. I can't describe half of what this thing was doing, but it was like having a little inanimate object seizure in my hand. I was a bit surprised, but thinking maybe heat was a factor and – I was, after all, the third one to try it – it had gotten warm, we let it cool on Adrienne's glass table.

We tried it again, me first this time, and it still would not calm down. I then handed it to Adrienne, and she passed it to my wife, and they still only got one response from the fish.

Still thinking body heat was a factor, we rolled up our shirts and tried our stomachs: no response from anyone. We tried Adrienne's chihuahua's stomach; no result. I held my glass of ice water, I switched hands, we turned off the electricity, changed places on the couch – but everything we tried yielded the same result. My fish was alive, while for them it was normal.

I don't know if I have some weird energies emanating from my hand or what. I realise that this toy is supposed to do something like this, to some extent, but has anyone else ever had an experience like this with one?
Alex -, by email, 2004

HUMAN AERIAL
I've always been able to "improve" the reception of televisions. I recall as a child, I learned the still-handy skill of being able to read no matter what was going on around me, because my parents would insist that I hang out in the family room, where they would watch the nightly news. Since these were the days before cable TV and our antenna was dicey in what it could pick up, having me there would ensure getting the broadcast they wanted, and Mom says it didn't matter what channel. I scarcely noticed, I always had my face in a book. I have three sisters and a brother – none of them has ever displayed the same, uh, talent. These days I can pick up a mobile phone in an area where there's generally no signal or too weak a signal to register, and I will get enough signal to place a call. Reassuring when driving at night on long lonely stretches of highway.
Anon, FTMB, 2003

COMPUTER CRASHER
I'm not allowed near my brother's nor my friends' palm-top computers because they break if I touch them (psions are more robust than palms – go figure). One of my best friends had to replace his. I interfere with computers, checkout machines, mobile phones (especially mobile phones) and other electrical equipment including radios when I'm stressed (or have had too much coffee and sugar). I can't wear a digital watch and analogue watches aren't much better unless they are clockwork. I can't tell if I interefere with the television because

we have Sky digital and it's pretty rubbish anyway. I really don't think that it's particularly unusual, although I did once come across a woman who claimed to be allergic to e-m radiation. And the colour red.

Out of interest, and to satisfy a vague idea, do any of you others reporting these effects have any food intolerances and if so, what are they?

Sam -, by email, 2003

THE ENGINEER'S CHAIR

A few weeks ago at the office, I was returning to my cubicle after a visit to the coffee machine. At the end of the hallway is the open office of one of our engineers. He's a pretty strange person: he mutters to himself, overreacts to the slightest provocation, and is generally regarded as an eccentric to whom you must be careful what you say.

He was sitting on a standard desk chair, leaning back. As I walked towards him, I had the strangest feeling, as if I was compelled to stare at him – or, more specifically, at his chair. Everything in my vision 'greyed out' except for Mr Engineer and his chair. All around me, the air felt tight or tense, almost as if there was an inaudible vibration centred around him.

PING!

A bolt shot out from the bottom of the chair, hitting the floor. The seatback rocked back, almost horizontal, nearly dumping him onto the floor. He grabbed the corner of his desk and shot a leg out to steady himself, now straddling the flopping item of furniture. In any other circumstance, I would have laughed, but I was amazed that I had 'felt' this event happen before it did. I returned to my cubicle, serenaded by a string of obscenities muttered under Mr Engineer's breath. Well, I'm assuming I just felt it – perhaps I'd actually caused the chair to break somehow by concentrating on it (although this would make me feel pretty guilty).

A little background: my fiancée is Pagan, so she's always talking about energies and things like that. I'm a pretty rational/scientific person, but I've studied martial arts and have learned about the Oriental philosophy of energy (chi). Surprisingly, the Pagan and Oriental ideas are compatible, and members of my class and my fiancée's group have done 'energy work' together. I'm still unclear as to how it all works, but I see more evidence of its truth every day.

B Steninger, Philadelphia, 2004

BEAM ME UP!

I WAS TELEPORTED!

A strange thing happened to me when I was 15 years old. We were on a family holiday and one night I awoke because my feet felt wet and cold. To my great surprise I was standing outside on the lawn, which was wet with dew.

"OK", I thought, "you sleepwalked out of the house". But when I tried to get back in, I found all the doors and windows closed. And they weren't just closed, they were locked. My mum had to unlock the front door to let me back in.

Anon, FTMB, 2003

FLYING FAMILY

My eldest sister tells a strange story from when she was perhaps six or seven years old. She had apparently climbed on top of a fence, and from there onto the roof of the house. Standing at a corner of the roof, she found herself wondering how she was going to get down again. She reports that she then found herself standing on the ground directly below where she had been on the roof, with no recollection of how she got there and no scrapes or bruises to suggest a fall. She just "got there" without knowing how.

My mother also tells a story about my sister. She was a young child, again about seven years old, and was skipping out the back door of the schoolhouse to the flight of steps leading to the playground. She then found herself floating above the playground, though no one else seemed to notice. A moment or two later she found herself a fair distance from the foot of the steps, again with no recollection of how she got there. Two flying women in one family it appears!

The best explanation I've heard for these stories is a momentary fugue state, where an individual is detached from his or her normal state of consciousness, but moving about in seemingly ordinary and businesslike fashion, only to return to consciousness a short while later, but with no recollection of any events during the passage of time.

Ian -, FTMB, 2002

FIFTY METRES IN A MOMENT

I had a similar experience as a child. I was standing on a verandah at school, when someone scared me from behind. A moment later, I was standing on the

> ❝ *Standing at a corner of the roof, she wondered how she would get down again* ❞

sports field some 50 metres (164ft) away, and everyone was staring at me, including a teacher.

All swore that I hadn't run – just vanished from one spot and appeared in the next! I don't know what the others thought, but I haven't forgotten it.

By the way, running would have been very slow for me anyway. The week before, I had caught my foot in the chain of my bicycle, and still had bandages and plaster on as it healed.

Perhaps – and this is just a theory – when we are truly scared or in the grip of some strong emotion, we can accomplish something that we can't in normal life.
Anon, FTMB, 2003

SAVED FROM A FALL

I grew up on a mountain in North Carolina and our main source of water was from an underground spring. My dad had rigged a pump device which he housed in an insulated box about 4ft by 4ft (1.2m by 1.2m), which itself stood on a concrete slab. A run-off hose emerged from the bottom of the slab, where excess water flowed down stone steps into a small pond.

One day, when I was about nine, my eldest brother was chasing me around; nothing too threatening, just horseplay. I jumped up on top of the pump house and began crawling backwards away from him until... I fell off! I hadn't considered running out of room! I went off head first, and had enough time to look "up" to see the concrete slab fast approaching. There was nothing else to do but shut my eyes tight and wait for impact.

After what seemed to be several seconds, I opened my eyes to find myself sitting in the middle of the stone steps, water flowing all around me – several feet from the run-off pipe. My hands were folded in my lap. Terrified, my brother came racing around the pump house – he said the last thing he saw was my legs going up in the air – to find me sitting and looking around dumbly. I remember when I got up, my pants weren't wet, although it took several seconds to figure out I wasn't dead!

Years later, while getting a haircut downtown, the barber asked where I lived. He said he knew that part of the mountain well; he used to play "hooky" up there and visit a very nice elderly couple. The man died peacefully under an apple tree, the remains of which were very close to the pump house.

As I said, I was nine. As the years went by, I started to doubt the thing had ever happened. I asked my brother about it, and he confirmed it to the last detail. I have no idea what or who saved me, but do know I made no physical effort to "pull out" of that head-first dive.

Tom Lev, by email, 2003

TELEPORTING MOTHER

When I was a young child my family was visiting my aunt and cousins at their farm in northern California. My eldest cousin and I had walked around one of the buildings and inadvertenly suprised a rattlesnake. David, my cousin, proved to be faster than the snake, and crushed its head with the heel of his boot.

We picked up the now inoperative snake and took in into the house. Upon seeing the snake my mother teleported from the floor to the top of a cabinet, at least 5ft (1.5m) from the floor. I was watching her for her reaction to the snake and have always been most impressed with this instantaneous movement.

The phenomenon, which I suspect is more general than suspected, seems to me to reflect a higher reality than we ususally perceive. What if our physical reality is only a projection of a higher one, and these teleportations are really a refocusing of that projection? It would be loosely analogous to defining a pixel of a particular colour at one point on a monitor then at the next moment redefining it at another. It would be at the new location, but would not appear to have moved across the screen.

Anon, FTMB, 2003

POWERS OF THE MIND

SPOONING

As a relatively inexperienced and unworldly 17-year-old boy, I had yet to develop a taste for Chinese food and so my choice was easy. The only English dish in the restaurant was Chicken Maryland, so that was that – with chips. I folded and re-placed the menu and gazed across the table. Joanne was more sophisticated than me in every way – she'd had rice before, even noodles, so she was taking her time to choose. As she studied the menu, I studied her. We were sitting at an intimate table for two at the Cherry Blossom restaurant in Acocks Green, Birmingham. It was the spring of 1981 and something quite inconsequential, but totally inexplicable was about to happen. Something I would remember for the rest of my life.

Joanne was a plump and bubbly girl who wore plump and bubbly glasses. Her most striking feature was her long sandy hair, which she parted in the centre and hooked over each ear. Not a classic beauty, but with her ready smile and cheerful personality, she was beautiful in my eyes. She was also the first girl I had had any kind of relationship with, so my feelings for her were quite intense. And I'm sure she liked me too. You could say there was a kind of bond between us, and that might go some way towards explaining what happened next.

I guess I was quite an immature young man, because as she looked down at the table I got the idea to pick up a spoon and tap her on her forehead. Why? I don't know. But I started to think about it in some detail. I imagined how the spoon would feel in my fingers. I imagined how the spoon's centre of gravity would be positioned between my thumb and forefinger and how it would feel to rock it back and forth. I then thought exactly how it would feel to gently rap her on the forehead. I considered the precise point of contact and how the impact would be transmitted down the shaft of the spoon to my fingers. And I also imagined what it would feel like for Joanne too. And I put all those thoughts together to create the complete mental event of the exact moment of impact of the spoon on her exposed brow.

At that exact moment, and to my complete and utter astonishment, Joanne suddenly looked up at me and asked, "Did you just hit me on the head with that spoon?"

I was so surprised that I didn't know what to say. I started to explain that I hadn't hit her but that I had been thinking about it. But as I spoke the words it sounded quite ridiculous to me, and by the look on Joanne's face she was finding it all quite confusing – and far-fetched too. So I let the event pass with a shrug of the shoulders and we got on with the rest of our evening. I cannot recall either of us mentioning it again. A few months later we parted company when Joanne went to university in Southampton and I went to Leeds.

That tiny moment happened nearly 30 years ago, but I have often thought about it and wondered what went on. Did we really have some kind of telepathic connection, or is there another explanation? Perhaps Joanne imagined I tapped her on the head and she asked that question just to check. Maybe, but unlikely. People don't just imagine they've been hit on the head – and what a co-inci-dence to imagine it as I was thinking it! Perhaps I actually did hit her on the head, and I somehow managed to only think I did it. Again, this is improbable – if she had been hit, she wouldn't need to ask, she'd know.

As I've thought about it over the years, I have come to believe that Joanne and I had an experience which cannot be explained by the common laws of nature. That's to say, it was a supernatural experience and it has convinced me that there is more to our existence than can be explained by the physical sci-ences. I've never talked about it or written about it before, and so I've no idea if anyone else has experienced anything similar, but I would be fascinated to find out.

Kevin Andrew, by email, 2009

PRIMÆVAL POWER

I work at a power station, and in about 1985 a colleague and I were working in some cooling voids – two large areas, each the size of a small house, linked by a high corridor at one end. A normally closed entrance door opened into one void on the corridor side. As it was pitch black in there, we had spotlights set up where we were working, but had finished in the void nearest the entrance and they were set up at the far void. This left the near void dark, with just enough light in the corridor to walk from the entrance.

Before entering the voids, we had to dress at a change barrier and on this day my colleague had entered a minute or so before me carrying some spare gloves, while I had a roll of tape. On opening the door, I saw no sign of him and assumed that he had reached the far void, which he could have easily done. However, as I walked along the edge of the near void heading for the corridor, I had a strange feeling and the hair on the back of my neck stood right up with a prickly sensation. I knew with absolute certainty that he was hiding in the darkness of the near void, and I turned and threw the roll of tape at where I thought he was standing.

He shouted out of the darkness and walked out of it towards me expressing great surprise that I could have known he was there and that the roll of tape had only missed him by six or eight feet (1.8–2.4m). He also said that he had kept perfectly quiet and had been about to throw the packet of gloves at me when I had thrown the tape at him. When I told him what had happened to me he thought it strange and we both laughed about it.

Looking back at it now I think it was the fact that he was effectively a predator – that is, about to attack me, if only with a packet of gloves – that triggered a primæval defence response. I had always thought that hairs standing up on the back of your neck was more a figure of speech until it actually happened but at least that is explicable, as when a cat meets a dog; but how I knew with such certainty exactly where he was has always mystified me.

Rupert Ell, Minehead, Somerset, 2009

7

Ghost Stories

Ghosts - whether they are spirits of the departed, supernatural replays of st events or misinterpretations of everyday phenomena - seem to come in as many different guises as do the people who report them. Here, we have family hauntings, friendly spirits, spooky children, terrifying apparitions and even a couple of cases in which the 'ghosts' have written in to identify themselves!

A SELECTION OF SPECTRES

CHILD REVENANT

A friend and work colleague recently bought a house in Worksop, Nottingham-shire, said to be over 300 years old, and began a steady programme of improvement, starting with the kitchen. Although a separate house, it was actually one third of a much larger farmhouse that had once been on the edge of town but had now been absorbed into the town as it grew. Of the three, his is effectively the 'left wing'.

He took an instant and intense dislike to a small bedroom; so did his 26-year-old daughter, who was also living there after her own flat purchase fell through. Neither could explain why. The room was drab and dark with only a small window letting in light. They decided to renovate this last, and in the meantime used it as a storeroom. They threw out a number of toys, damaged children's books, and a rickety wardrobe to create some space and make the best of what natural light there was. Even so, the room still left them both with a sense of unease. What's more, 'Duchess' the family mongrel, a generally happy animal ready to lick and slaver over all and sundry, refused to go anywhere near the room or for that matter the cellar – a favourite haunt of my friend's as he keeps his extensive wine and beer collection there.

Some weeks later, my friend's daughter went on a girls' night out to celebrate her team completing the Great North Run in aid of Breast Cancer Research. To her surprise, the main turn of the evening was a clairvoyant. I say surprise because it was supposed to be cabaret night. She is a strong 'unbeliever' in such things and openly sceptical, but sat back to enjoy the show. I should point out that she is a pharmacist, not given to flights of fancy. Unfortunately, the show involved her, almost from the off. The clairvoyant singled her out and made a series of statements so accurate and impressive that she had to have the next day off work with the shock.

He told her that she had just moved house, and disliked a small room facing east. The reason for this was that the room had a ghost, a small child. She had heard the child crying, and had wrongly assumed it was the neighbour's baby – but while the neighbours have children, they have no baby. The child, a girl, was waiting for its parents to pass over (which suggests they are still alive) and was concerned about her toys which she wanted back, specifically 'the horses' which my friend's daughter realised were two broken toy unicorns that had been thrown away the previous week. The child also said that she watched every night as my friend's daughter read herself to sleep and wondered what it was she was reading as it looked interesting; and by the way could she have her baby books back? There were also comments about the colour of the rooms, wiring, potential problems with the fireplace (which as she stated was built into the house and embedded in bedrock) and choice of covering for the kitchen floor.

All of these and more proved to be entirely accurate, most impressively the colour of the room that was haunted. Through the clairvoyant, the child asked for it "not to be painted red again", a puzzle as the room was wallpapered and the paper painted mushroom. Even peeling back the layers of paper showed no hint of red – until it came to painting the doorframe. There, above the frame, almost imperceptible, was a thin line of red, the original colour. What she found most disconcerting was the concept of being observed.

None of this moved my friend much; in fact, having smartened up the room, he rented it out to a female friend, although in fairness he did tell her of the room's recent history. The new lodger, a shop manager, took it all very seriously and went to the trouble of bringing in books and toys for the ghost, and took to wishing it goodnight. Touchingly, she even left some Christmas cake – which was left untouched. The net result is that the gloom that enveloped the room has been lifted, and even the dog is now prepared tentatively to enter the room (though not the cellar); but there was one small coda.

My friend – who incidentally has neither seen nor felt anything apart from his initial dislike of the room – likes a drink on a Friday night, and coming home tipsy one evening felt a great urge to open the door of the bedroom. In fact he couldn't stop himself, and wasn't happy until he'd gone upstairs, opened it and spragged it open for good measure. He then realised why – the toys and books had been turfed out and left on the landing by his mother who had popped in to tidy up. The ghost had 'suggested' to him that he either put them back or opened the door to give her access.

Shortly after this, the lodger/girlfriend was taken aback to see her collection of small perfume atomisers neatly lined up in order of size, and her collection of Steiff bears all gently turned round and positioned so they could see out of the window. It seems that the phantom child has a tidy mind.

At a party, the group in the house mentioned the presence of a ghost to one of the guests, who happened to have an interest in the occult and was one of a group who took 'astral photos' that showed up golden globes. Without further ado, she went upstairs with her camera and began snapping furiously in the dark, at which 'a force' threw her down a flight of stairs (a fair amount of drink was involved) – but her photos showed not one, but dozens of orbs of various sizes.

It appears that this little ghost is confined to that room and its immediate environs but can nevertheless see or sense everything that goes on in the house, a kind of prison with a roving panorama. The clairvoyant has since contacted them to offer his services in helping the ghost to move on, but frankly the three in the house have grown used to it and feel quite protective towards her. I have been sworn to the utmost secrecy regarding the identity of those involved, as the whole thing sounds a bit far-fetched and they might want to sell the house in due course, even though the ghost told them they would live there a long time and be very happy. My father knew one of the previous owners of the house, but he could throw no light on the haunting; he did say, however, that the house had been sold very cheaply several times in quick succession.

Jack Romano, by email, 2011

VANISHING MAN

My first sighting of a ghost (I can't think what else to call it) was in about 1955, when I was 15 years old. I used to go to a model aircraft club in downhill Lincoln and my mother always insisted I was home "before the pubs turn out" (10pm in those days). So I left the club at about 9.30 and was pushing my bike up the very steep Spring Hill when I saw a man lying in the gutter. My first thought was that he was a drunk, and I was scared, but he held up his arm as if asking for help, and looked injured. He was wearing "old fashioned" clothes: a light brown overcoat with very wide lapels and tight black trousers. He opened his mouth as if trying to speak, but there was no sound. I hurried past, and then after going about five paces I thought I should see if I could help him. I leant my bike in the doorway of Spring Hill School (it's modern flats now) and turned round but there was no one there. The gutter was empty.

When I arrived home I told my parents about seeing him. It had really scared me. My mother said he was most likely drunk. Next morning I thought I had dreamed it and told my mother again, but she said that I had told her the previous evening.

Michael Fletcher, by email, 2010

THE FIGURE AT THE TABLE

The most alarming experience I had in the 1930s house where I grew up in Titirangi, Auckland, New Zealand, was late one Friday night sometime in 1991 or 1992, when I was around 14. My mother was a teacher and had borrowed a VHS video camera from her school to do some filming at the weekend. Once everyone had retired, I set the camera up on a tripod in the centre of the lounge, pointing down onto the floor. I intended to record some tests of filming photographs onto video, and dubbing sound on at a later stage in order to create a video slide show. I experimented for some time with this, recording short sections and trying fades, zooms etc. After a while, on a whim, I decided to turn the camera up and look at the room through the viewfinder, which was black and white. I started at one side and panned from right to left. On the left side of the room, the lounge became the dining room, connected by a wide doorway.

As I panned the camera around, I was looking through the viewfinder the entire time. Seated at the end of the table was a black figure, facing not towards me but probably at 45 degrees. The figure consisted of a featureless black body, with no discernible arms, and a black head that was also blank and featureless except for two white eyes. I was stunned for a moment, then took my eye off the viewfinder and looked into the dining room. There was no figure there. Returning to the viewfinder, the figure was no longer visible. I was the only person awake at the time. As I had been working for quite a while on my slide show I estimate the time was probably between midnight and 1am. I decided to pack the camera away and retire for the night. The figure I observed through the viewfinder was truly remarkable, and I regret I was not filming at the time. There was a blank videotape in the camera, but I had decided simply to pan around without recording.

Adam McGechan, Auckland, New Zealand, 2004

GHOSTS IN THE FAMILY

GRANDFATHERLY SPIRIT

Two years ago my granddad died. My grandmother was afraid to go back to her house alone because it was the first time ever she had been without him. My great aunt came down to offer moral support and to stay with her so my grandmother could get used to the house again. The first night they slept there, they kept hearing knocking – angry knocking – from downstairs. My great aunt went to check, but there was no one there. The knocking carried on every night until my great aunt left, and then stopped. My granddad had said many years before, after a family argument, that he didn't want my great aunt in the house ever again. We assumed he was still around in spirit and hadn't forgiven her.

My uncle moved into the house, and my grandmother moved in with us. He told us that the knocking had started up again. It wasn't just confined to the house, though. I was staying at my boyfriend's flat. One night I was woken by a violent knocking on the bathroom door, which was beside the bed and had swung open. I asked my boyfriend if he'd heard it; he had, but assumed it was just the wind. He later admitted that there was no way the wind could have caused the noise and he knew the door had been shut properly, as he had closed it himself. We also started to smell my granddad's aftershave quite often. I smelt it, and so did my mother. This occurred at her house, my boyfriend's flat, and even at my university halls, many miles away!

My grandmother died later that year. The knocking and banging stopped. We no longer smelt aftershave. It seems to us that my granddad was warning us about her impending illness and was waiting for her.

Name withheld, by email, 2001

CHOP CHOP

It was a summer night and my cousins and I were spending a few weeks in our family's hamlet in the mountains. I woke up in the middle of the night to the sound of steps outside the house, and the sound of wood being chopped. Feeling curious, I looked through the window, but it was a dark night and I couldn't see a thing. As I stared towards the woods, I noticed I could also hear heavy breathing. I thought it must be a wild boar, or even a wolf or a bear cub – after all, it wouldn't have been the first time.

The following morning, while we were all having breakfast, I was telling the others about my story. One of my cousins, who slept in a different room, told me that he had also woken up at the same time, feeling unusually cold, and that he too had heard the sound of wood being chopped and heavy breathing coming from outside.

Our great-aunt, who was in the kitchen with us, joined the conversation. She said she believed that it had to do with one of our ancestors whom we hadn't known: he was a woodcutter... and he suffered from asthma. The previous night, she went on to tell us, had been the anniversary of his death.

J Pérez, Asturias, Spain, 2010

MATERNAL CRISIS APPARITION

Last year my mother was unfortunate enough to contract Legionnaire's Disease and spent several weeks in hospital. For the majority of this time she was sedated with morphine and completely unconscious. Her illness was so bad that her family and friends were prepared for the worst.

As the disease took an increasingly powerful hold over my mother, people around her started to experience strange things. Her next-door neighbour, who is a good friend, was in her back garden one day bending down to pull weeds out of the ground. She was suddenly aware of a presence next to her and looked up to see my mum standing nearby watching her work. The image vanished but not before the neighbour had time to get a good look at my mum and even recognise the clothes that she was wearing, (not the nightie that she was actually wearing in hospital but some of her ordinary clothes).

A few days after this, my auntie was also visited by my mother in her house and once again was able to get a very clear view of her before the image disappeared. As before, my mum was just standing beside her appearing to take an interest in what my auntie was doing.

" *He heard the sound of wood being chopped and heavy breathing* "

Typically, I was one of the few people who never saw this ghostly image of my mother but she did visit me in other ways. After visiting her in the hospital, I would come home to find the TV switched on (I had definitely switched it off before leaving the house) and it would be busily changing channels by itself. It would also have the annoying habit of switching channels in the middle of the programme I was watching.

A few days after the visions mentioned above, my other half was relaxing in the bath one evening when suddenly he had an overwhelming urge to get out and stand in the middle of the bathroom. He did this and was rewarded with the sound of a loud groan, which he was sure came from my mother. He told me that it felt as though she wanted to tell him that things had changed and she was going to be OK.

We later found out that it was about this time that my mother suddenly stopped getting worse. Within a few days she even began to get better and has now thankfully made a full recovery.

She has no memory of her various apparitions but says that the morphine produced many hallucinations and bizarre dreams. As soon as she regained full consciousness the problems with my TV stopped and have never happened since. It seems strange that someone can appear as a ghost whilst still living, but I feel that the severity of my mother's illness and the huge amount of morphine that she was given (the hospital gave her extra doses in the expectation that she was not going to pull through) combined to allow her to leave her body in spirit form and visit those closest to her.

This has, however, left my boyfriend with the worrying impression that when my mother does finally shuffle off the mortal coil, neither of us will get a moment's peace.

Alison Derrick, Herefordshire, 2003

A LIFETIME'S GHOSTS

My grandfather, who walked with a limp, died before I was born. One night, my uncle babysat me while my parents went out. When they came home, I was lying in my cot in the front bedroom upstairs. Suddenly there were thudding noises across the landing, like someone walking with a limp, and my dad was convinced it sounded like my grandfather's footsteps.

When I was small, I used to share a bedroom with my sister. Every time I was poorly, she would take me into my mum's room. One night I wasn't feeling very well, and my mum woke up to see me standing at the foot of her bed with a young girl, who had her arms around me. She thought my sister had taken me into her room, but she hadn't. Mum took her eyes off me for a second and the girl had gone.

I was lying in bed one night aged about 10 when I saw my mongrel dog Candy, who was run over when I was eight and was buried in the garden. She rolled up in a ball and fell asleep, and then she vanished. I can clearly remember sitting in an empty form room at school with a friend, when I felt something tugging hard at the front of my jacket. It was as if someone wanted my attention, and the tugging persisted until I told my friend what was happening. She was so scared she ran out of the classroom.

I was still seeing ghosts at the age of 17. One night, I woke up with a start in the early hours and when I turned over, I saw a male figure, matching the description of my grandfather, standing by the bedside. I couldn't see the background, as everything was white around him. He stood there for a few seconds, then went away.

One cold January morning recently, I was visiting Ulverscroft Manor, a 300-year-old country manor house in Charnwood Forest, Markfield, Leicestershire, with a group of wheelchair users from Rawlins College in Quorn. When we arrived, we went into the lounge and sat in a semi-circle around the fire. I glanced up and noticed a blur in between two wheelchairs as large as life! It was a young boy dressed in a grey blazer with short grey trousers and white tights.

He was standing sideways to me, looking away from me, and was surrounded with a white mist. As I looked at him, he disappeared into thin air suddenly, leaving me looking at the floor, feeling somewhat overwhelmed but elated, not scared. It gave me a sense of privilege to have seen him. I wrote to the chief executive of Ulverscroft Manor and told him about what I had seen. He replied that over the past few years people had sensed a bad presence upstairs on the landing.

Sometimes I have felt the presence of ghosts without actually seeing them. For example, in the middle of the night, in bed, I have sometimes felt that my dad (who died six years ago) was there, putting his arms around me in a kind of reassuring way.

Another time, I awoke in the night to find a monk standing at the bottom of my bed. Two weeks later, I was admitted to the Royal Infirmary. I think that the monk was a warning sign.

All that I experienced and witnessed seemed very apparent to me but not to others.

Hayley Smith, Anstey, Leicestershire, 2010

Hayley Smith is 40 years old. She suffers from Friedreich's Ataxia (diagnosed at the age of 10) and is almost completely paralysed. In particular, she has great difficulty in speaking. She lost her mobility when she was a teenager. The above account was transcribed by Morry van Ments, who works with the Ryder-Cheshire Volunteers.

ECCENTRIC APPARITIONS

THE NIXON CHANNEL

Back in 1994, I wrote the first account of the haunting of the Nixon Library, noting poltergeist-like phenomena in three areas of the facility: the Nixon Birthplace house, Nixon's grave, and the Watergate display. At the Birthplace, a night watchman reported seeing a ghostly figure enter the house through a locked door. Over Nixon's grave, a hovering green mist had been observed. And in the original Watergate display area (which has since been renovated), tapping sounds were heard and the tape machines were in frequent disrepair. (According to the medium Dorothy Maksym, quoted in the book *The Haunting of the*

Presidents, the tapping sound was Nixon's way of distracting visitors, to keep them from concentrating on the Watergate materials.) Years later, according to Maksym, the channelled ghost of Nixon described, in detail, someone who could only be me as the original witness to the grave's green mist. Through Maksym, Nixon went on to state that his "spirit is working" through me – which came as quite a disturbing surprise!

On a recent sunny Sunday afternoon, I conducted a ghost tour through the Nixon Library & Birthplace along with famed medium Joseph Ross, known for his many radio and television appearances since the 1960s. Our group of 14 arrived at the Nixon Library in Yorba Linda, California, about 30 miles (48km) southeast of downtown Los Angeles. Dressed all in black and wearing a necklace with a large crystal pendant, Joseph Ross looked like a cross between a priest and a 19th-century magician. As the group toured the massive facility, Ross continually channelled Nixon, who would comment on various aspects of the displays. Just beyond the museum entrance are cases of artefacts from Nixon's early life, prior to his entering politics – grade school essays, early photographs, love letters to Pat and Naval service documents. Here, the spirit of Nixon told the group that this was the only part of the library that he still enjoyed visiting.

We moved on to the Hall of World Leaders, which features life-size statues of Chairman Mao, Khrushchev, Brezhnev, Sadat, Churchill and others. Here, two members of our group reported strange buzzing sounds in their ears, as if caused by insects, but none was found. At various locations, many in our group reported a nauseating smell whose origin could not be determined. It seemed to follow us throughout the day.

We arrived at the Watergate display area, which was renovated in 2007, some believe in the hope of exorcising whatever force was causing the tape machines to malfunction. Many in the group immediately felt an unearthly chill. We searched for an air conditioning duct, but found nothing. For the library's first 17 years, the original Watergate display was a really creepy, dimly lit corridor that exhibited photographs of the Watergate burglars and their tools. It also had a row of tape players with headphones where visitors could listen to copies of the Watergate tapes.

Unfortunately, the newly remodelled Watergate display is lacklustre and feels almost like a shameful afterthought. The wall is painted an institutional olive drab colour, with the bank of large, interactive monitors all out of order.

" We gathered beside Nixon's grave, formed a circle and all joined hands "

Perhaps Nixon's troubled spirit hasn't left the area.

Next, we went outside to the birthplace house. The tour guide said that although he had heard reports of the haunting of the house, he had not witnessed any phenomena. He posited that perhaps it was not Nixon haunting the house, but the spirit of a later inhabitant. Inside the house, Joseph Ross said that this is where he feels Nixon's spirit most strongly, and that Nixon visits his birthplace every night.

It was getting late. One of the security guards informed us that the library was about to close for the day, so we gathered beside Nixon's grave, formed a circle and all joined hands as Ross did his final channelling. The Sun was low in the sky, casting our shadows dramatically across Nixon's grave. Ross said that after many years of turmoil, Nixon's spirit was now considerably more at peace. With several security guards observing, I was trying to imagine who they thought we were. We must have looked like either some kind of fundamentalist prayer group, or some weird cult. As we released hands, everyone in the group was surprised to be overcome by a warm, peaceful sensation.

Before departing, I reached down and scooped up soil from Nixon's grave, which I have since preserved in several small glass vials, one of which I preserved in a reliquary which I keep close at all times.

Jeffrey Vallance, Los Angeles, California, 2009

BORED SPOOK

My flatmate was standing in my room talking to me, and I was switching looking between him and the computer screen, as we were watching a music video (Johnny Cash's version of 'Hurt') while talking. I looked round at him, and there was a man standing behind him. My face dropped and the apparition faded. I was literally lost for words.

It only lasted for about half a second, but my flatmate instantly said, "Did you see a man?" and I said yes. Apparently, he'd seen him the night before, and the ghostie had said he'd follow him around for a few days because he was bored. (I'm not making this up, but my flatmate might have done.)

My flatmate seems particularly 'conducive' to this sort of thing. The only three potential spooks I've ever seen (this one, a walking torso and a genuine orb) were in his presence.
Taras Young, Edinburgh, Scotland, 2004

I WAS A WARTIME GHOST!

In spite of experiencing a number of queer happenings during my life (84 next birthday), I have never seen a ghost. I can claim, however, to have been one myself. It happened on 21 September 1943, during World War II. At that time, there was still a threat of air raids, so fire-watch duties were still undertaken. Mine was at the University, Edgbaston, Birmingham. If the night proved quiet, at a time well past midnight the custom, for those who wished, was to go home. My own home was a walk of some four or five miles (6-8km) away, in Handsworth. My route took me past an old church that had a yard reputedly haunted, odd noises coming from it at midnight on the Autumn Equinox. Since the country was observing double summer time, midnight occurred at 2am.

So I arrived at the churchyard a few minutes early, climbed over the lych gate and made my way to the grave that was supposed to be the centre of the haunting. It was a fine, balmy night with a trace of moonlight. Minutes passed; nothing. Then I heard a faint, puffing, snuffling sort of noise that gradually grew louder. I couldn't place it, and it sounded like no animal I knew. It was soon joined by another noise, a high-pitched squeak – puff, squeak, puff, squeak, puff. I became seriously alarmed, and the hairs on my neck began to prickle.

I was about to make a run for it, when the source of the noise came into view – a man, riding a squeaky bike, puffing as he pushed the pedals. I burst out laughing – relief – but he didn't stop to investigate. Putting his head over the handlebars, he pedalled away as fast as he could. So for me the haunting on that night was a myth, but not, I suspect, for him. How else to explain, at that time and place, a shriek of near-hysterical laughter?

Well, I thought it was funny – still do, 65 years later.

Colin Reid, Admaston, Shropshire, 2008

AND I WAS THE CEMETERY SNOW-SPOOK!

A few New Year's Eves ago I was walking home from the pub and decided to take a short cut through the cemetary (as you do when a bit drunk!). It was a really cold winter with about an inch of snow on the ground and, naturally, I fell over – leaving a perfect "person print" on the grass behind me.

Well, a few days later a letter appeared in the local paper from a man saying he was walking through the cemetary and saw this human-shaped indentation in the snow – he was convinced he had evidence of a soul rising from the grave! There were even follow-up letters from other people saying they had seen it too and a short discussion about how there were footprints leading away from the figure (nobody seemed to notice the footprints leading to it).

I wrote to the editor to explain, but they never printed my letter!

Jane -, by email, 2002

8 Dog-Headed Men

One of the strangest of strange phenomena to have emerged from the *Fortean Times* message boards has been the truly bizarre saga of the Dog-Headed Men – unfeasible-sounding entities that crop up everywhere from Manchester to Massachusetts to Malaysia and beyond, spreading confusion and terror in their wake. Please report straight to *FT* if you see any prowling about *your* neighbourhood...

NORTHERN DOG-HEADS

THE 'BIG DOGS' OF STATION STREET

In the late 1960s we lived in Station Street, Crewe, which we left when the whole area was to be slum-cleared. The houses were old-fashioned – very basic terraces opening directly onto the street – and as everyone knew everyone else it was safe to 'play out' quite late at night. One evening, my brother Mark (aged about nine) was walking along the wide pavement when he saw some characters coming toward him. There were three, I think, and they were somewhat taller than people.

They were dressed as men in suits, but had very large dogs' heads! These heads swayed widely from side to side as the creatures walked. Mark was absolutely terrified as they approached, but they seemed not to notice him and he passed them safely. He ran all the way home and only told me about the 'Big Dogs' as he called them some time later. I laughed my head off, thinking he was trying to scare me. When it became obvious that he was really frightened, I tried to figure out what he'd seen. My 10-year-old brain could only come up with ghosts or aliens, neither of which seemed to fit the bill.
Carla R, FTMB, 2001

DOG-HEADS IN MANCHESTER

Reading the story about the dog-headed men reminds me of a similar thing that happened to me as a child of about 10. I used to live in a place called Ashton, in east Manchester. Behind our house there were two large factories, and while playing down there one summer morning my friend (who was the same age as me) told me to look at two figures who were walking towards us, silhouetted against the Sun. We thought it was our parents coming to tell us off for playing where we shouldn't, but when the figures got closer one of them appeared to have a dog's head.

We froze, completely still. It was obvious that it was a real dog's head due to the detail that was visible and the way it moved; the other figure was human.

We both ran home and told our parents. They didn't believe us, but they could see that we were genuinely spooked and called the police. A few hours later, they caught up with a man whom we identified as the one we'd seen with the dog-headed figure.

He told the police that what we had described was true, and claimed he had met the dog-man on the banks of the canal and was following him to see if he was real. He claimed that he had lost him at some point, but neither the police nor our parents believed this story. To this day, nobody has believed me, so to hear of a similar account is amazing!
Anon, FTMB, 2001

LEATHER-HEADS

In Yorkshire folklore, they were called 'leather-heads', due to the fact that from a distance they looked as if they were wearing leather flaps when it was actually their ears. They always caused a nuisance when they turned up. My grandfather used to tell me about them as a lad. Apparently, they were to be seen mostly around the north-western side of Barnsley between Hoyland and Holmfith, and in Penistone, Huddersfield, and Glossop way.
Anon, FTMB, 2002

FOX-FACE AT THE WINDOW

My friend saw a dog-faced man. When she was about 13 (she's 32 now) she was in the lounge at her parents' house in Gatley (in Stockport, Cheshire) with a boyfriend who was staying the night. Her parents had gone to bed, and she was about to go upstairs herself, leaving the boyfriend to sleep in the lounge. They were saying goodnight and both passed in front of the lounge window. Through a gap in the curtains they both saw a tall man in a long black cloak with what she described to me as the head of a fox.

They were terrified, and she couldn't bring herself to go upstairs for ages, as she would have to pass the window again. They discussed what they had seen and agreed that they had definitely seen the same thing. She never told her parents, and to this day doesn't have a clue what it could have been.

Ever the sceptic, I told her it was probably a fox standing on the garden wall and that a trick of the light made the surrounding wall look like a cloak. Well, that's what I'd like to think it was anyway. The other option is far too scary!
Stargazeypie, FTMB, 2003

THE PEOPLE'S PARK DOG-MAN

As a child growing up in Grimsby in the late 1970s, my walk to school took me through People's Park. It was well known amongst local children that a dog-man lived in the park. I saw him once, although my memory of the encounter is hazy. One thing I do remember thinking is, wow, he really does look like a dog! He had huge purple jowls that hung down on either side of his face. And he even barked at me!

With hindsight, the explanation for this encounter is probably an unfortunately disfigured individual scaring away hostile children.
Suzy Blue, FTMB, 2004

ON THE PROWL

PACED IN THE PARK

A friend of mine called Mark claimed to have been paced by a dog-headed man across Kings Norton Green Park in Birmingham a number of years ago. He said he thought it was a man in fancy dress at first, but realised the motion was too fluid to be someone with a dog mask on. He also saw breath coming from the end of its snout. It was late at night. The creature was very tall – approximately 7-8ft (2-2.4m) in height. Mark said it never looked at him or approached him, but kept a straight course parallel to his; when he ran, the creature ran too, but again on

a parallel course keeping level with him. It really freaked him out, and to my knowledge I'm the only person he has ever told (knowing my interest in weird experiences). I never walked across the park at night after that and have often wondered what it might have been. Of course, one can never rule out drugs or alcohol, but Mark was a pretty straight guy and not one for tall stories.
Rich -, by email, 2003

BLACK PAD

I was having a conversation with a friend the other night. He told me that as a child he had seen what he described as "a black dog the size of a man walking on its hind legs" through a park in Coventry.

What's really interesting about this is the fact that the park where he saw his dog-headed man was very close to an alleyway called Black Pad, which is allegedly haunted by Coventry's very own phantom Black Dog, also called Black Pad!
Piers L, by email, 2006

BARE-ASSED DOG-HEAD

A childhood friend and I ran into a dog-headed man once, out in the woods of Mashpee, Massachusetts, a little town on Cape Cod. (I like to call it Monster Island; not for fortean reasons, but family ones!)

It was winter, and we had been up to no good in the nearby cranberry bogs and woods that separated our town from a nearby military base (Camp Edwards/Otis Air Force Base). As twilight descended, we started back home, throwing rocks at ice formations, yelling, generally carrying on like the kids that we were, when we heard a distinct "cough" sound behind us.

We both turned around to see a very large, strange man-like creature crouched on a nearby dirt mound, watching us. He was a tall bugger – even crouched, he was taller than us (we were 10 and 11 years old). He had what appeared to be the head of a German Shepard, and he was completely bare-assed! In the winter! Needless to say, we both screamed like six-year-old girls and ran as fast as our crazy little legs would carry us!

Talking about it later, we both remarked on how strange its eyes were. The rest of the head seemed natural enough – we both saw its lips move in the sneering way that a dog's would – but the eyes were very weird, very black. They had an almost bug-like look to them, as if they were multifaceted. Perhaps a better description would be that they looked like microphone covers, or some form of

> *They saw the shadowy figure of a man, but with a dog's head, moving rapidly*

screening.

I know this makes it sound like a mask, and that was what we ended up convincing ourselves it was – a mask. Yet, I still wonder...
Trace Mann, by email 2003

VERY BAD FENG SHUI

I'd like to share the story of my two brothers' close encounter with a dog-headed man.

They were both in their early teens when, one night at about 8pm, they went out for a walk. On the way home, they decided to take a closer look at the fine new two-storey villa being constructed opposite our house. They walked up the drive and peered into the front window – and were both amazed to see the shadowy figure of a man, wearing a patterned shirt and dark trousers, but with a dog's head. It was moving rapidly, with a stiff gait, like someone walking on tiptoe, from the kitchen towards the staircase – the back door had not been installed, so perhaps it came in from the forest at the back of the site into the half completed house. The figure was clearly silhouetted in the doorway for a few moments before it disappeared. The street was very well lit, and the inside of the house was clearly visible with well-defined shadows. Feeling totally creeped-out, they left quickly. The older brother drew a picture of what he saw. Our mother took a look and exclaimed in hushed tones: "A dog-headed elemental!" (She actually used a Chinese term, but that's how I would translate it).

Actually the house had very bad feng shui, being sited on top of a T-junction with the middle stem of the 'T' leading directly to the front door. Also, it was too close to the forest, so as well as visitors of the paranormal kind, there were those of the furry and scaly kind.

There were some peculiar happenings after the house was finished and the owners moved in. The first week, we and the other neighbours were disturbed nightly at about 11pm by the owners' black Labrador dog howling, to be followed at about 1am by their toddler son's terrified screams! Of course, we couldn't go up and knock on their front door and ask if anybody had seen a dog-headed figure...

Well, the next thing we noticed was the local priest conducting a house blessing ceremony – or was it an exorcism? Not being Catholic I couldn't tell, but I recognised the priest – an old Dutch guy with long flowing beard. After that, all was quiet, but the owners moved out after a short while.

Much later one brother was reading a book on the pyramids and yelped, "Look! That's what it was! Anubis!" So there you have it – dog-headed men are a global phenomenon!

I should point out that this brother is famous in the family for encounters of the supernatural kind. He used to travel a bit on his job and his more memorable experiences included a ghostly nun or nurse in a 16th-century Dutch building, the ghostly footsteps of a suicide in a government rest house and a hair-pulling entity in a seaside bungalow... but there were no more dog-headed men!
Elsie L, Malaysia, 2004

DOG-HEADED MEN ON CAMPUS

In 1984 I was at computer camp at the University of Maine at Machias. A bunch of us girls were sitting in one of our second floor rooms. It was sometime in the afternoon, with clear visibility. All of a sudden, one of the girls freaked out, saying that she had seen an ape in the woods, and another girl claimed to have seen it just before it disappeared. I didn't see anything; I just happened to be there.

A couple of days later, I was sitting in the lounge when three of the boys came running in, seemingly panicked. Dave, one of my childhood best friends and not prone to making things up, was the most disturbed, and he immediately shut and locked all the windows, despite it being a hot summer's night.

Eventually, we got them to tell us what had happened. Apparently, they were outside the dorm (it was after dark, so they weren't supposed to be), having sneaked out a window, when Dave suddenly flipped out, grabbed the other two boys one after the other and threw them back in the window – and he wasn't a particularly strong kid. According to Dave, he suddenly saw a big, hairy, man-like thing with the head of a dog and glowing eyes. He claims it was at least nine feet tall. (Dave has always been kind of tall, so even at age 12 if he thought something was tall, it probably was). That's when he freaked out and hoiked everyone in through the window. Once again, I never saw the thing myself, but I was the one to connect the two stories.

Anon, FTMB, 2004

IN THE WOODS

I thought I saw something similar to this when I was seven. It was in the after-noon in the woods near a house that we were all scared of. I thought I saw what looked like someone in a trench coat with a canine head. It was dark in the wooded area and I was looking in over the fence, I didn't see any detail or colour but I thought I saw pointy dog/wolf type ears on the clothed body. I thought I heard growling as well, which was confirmed by my friend.

We ran as fast as we could and locked ourselves in my friend's garage, too scared to open it up for 20 minutes.

Anon, FTMB, 2004

DOG-HEADED BURGLAR?

Reading these stories reminded me of a related story that had happened to my brother a few years back. He would have been 18-19, and he awoke one night with a severe case of the munchies. Heading into the kitchen, he glanced out of the little window set in the door leading to the porch and noticed the back door was wide open. So he unlocked the kitchen door, walked through the porch and was about to close the back door when he was attacked from behind. He was hit in the back of the head and pushed violently to one side as the attacker bolted for freedom. Landing on the washing machine, he managed to stay upright and get a good look at the figure as it took a running jump over the 4ft (1.2m) gate of our garden. He thought it was a burglar, until he noticed what appeared to be fox-like or wolf-like ears on its head, and an elongated snout as it turned its head slightly to look back at him.

He passed it off as an hallucination brought on by the blow to the back of his head. A likely story!

Anon, FTMB, 2004

WISCONSIN WOLF-PEOPLE

Although not strictly dog-related, an American friend I knew while at college many moons ago told me a pretty weird story that he had been told by his girl-friend (who was of Native American descent). According to this story, her grand-father had seen and shot at several creatures that looked like wolves... only they walked on their hind legs. More distinct details escape me, but she did say that such creatures were part of the local Wisconsin folklore.

Jerry B, FTMB, 2002

THE MAN WITH FLOPPY EARS

I once saw what I believe to be a dog-headed man in Guildford about three years ago. He was kind of like a basset hound, with long floppy ears. He crossed my path a short distance in front of me, so I only saw him from the side. I always put it down to imagination, but now that others are reporting the same thing I wonder if it was real.

Kate -, Ipswich, Suffolk, 2002

DOG-HEADS ON THE ROAD

CAUGHT IN THE HEADLIGHTS

I live in the eastern part of Tennessee. I work second shift at a factory about 25 miles (40km) from my home and travel a mountain road to and from work. One night, about 1.30am, I was on my way home. I wasn't a bit tired; in fact, I was very awake and alert. Up ahead, my headlights picked up a man walking toward me on the side of the road. As I got closer, he turned his back to me and bent forward. As I passed, he peered around to look toward me and I saw he had the head of a dog! It looked like a Great Dane, although he had human clothing on. I jumped out of my skin! I looked in my rear-view mirror, but as it was so dark I couldn't see anything.

Pat Law, by email, 2006

DOG-HEAD AT THE WHEEL

More than 10 years ago, my son and his father both saw a man with a dog's head

driving a van down the high street. They said it was so realistic that it must have been some fancy animatronic mask. It was brown, and somewhere between a Doberman and a Labrador in type. It was looking forward, quite calmly, not trying to draw attention to itself.
Marion-, FTMB, 2002

DHM DOUBLE-TAKE

I had to do a double take the other day. As I was walking away from a cash dispenser I heard a car engine rev up and saw a basset hound at the driving wheel of a parked car, with a paw at each side of the wheel. It appeared to be looking in the wing mirror prior to driving off. It turned out to be the car behind that was pulling away, but it gave me quite a turn. I've obviously been reading too many dog-headed men stories!
butterfly27, FTMB, 2002

TRANSFORMATIONS

DOG-HEADED DATE FROM HELL

When I was a rebellious teenager of about 15 (though I looked much older) I met a guy in his late 20s at a mediæval party – one of those where folks pretend to be from the Middle Ages, complete with costumes, food and even slave auctions. Anyhow, this guy was very charismatic – everyone seemed to be attracted to him and wanted his attention. He told folks that he practised ancient magic, like Merlin. What was most amazing to me at the time was that this guy seemed to have complete control over others – like a hypnotic power – and they would do anything he asked. At the party, he focused on me, and was determined to date me. I told him no, I was too young for him, and my parents would kill me.

Fast forward a month or so, and this guy was still trying to get me to date him. He'd call my house, try to get my friends to set up a date, show up at my high school events and so on. He seemed to know everything about me, and tried to be where I would be. I still said no. He was starting to freak me out so badly that I told my parents about him. However, they had never met him and didn't know what he looked like.

One day, while I was at school, this guy came by the house, pretending to be selling something. My mom answered the door, told him no, and then went back to cleaning the house. We always left the door unlocked, and he must've then come back and gotten into the house, because, later when I came home from school, there was a note from him on my bed. I asked my mom if this guy had come by, and then my mom told me about the salesman and we figured out that he was my stalker.

Later, in the middle of the night, there was a knock at our door. I was dead asleep, and never heard a thing. My dad went to the door, and there was my stalker. He demanded to see me, told my dad I was "his" – and that was it. My dad told him to f**k off, and never come back again, and started out the door to physically remove the guy from our property. At that point, the guy transformed himself into a dog-headed man, said something in another language, and then vanished into thin air.

My dad went inside, locked every door and window, woke up my mom, and told her the story. He was shaken and pale, frightened to death, she said. They didn't go back to sleep that night. When I woke up, he and my mom told me what had happened, and they described my stalker exactly. My dad was never a religious man, but he believed he'd seen the Devil or a demon coming for his daughter. It scared him enough that he agreed that my mom should call the ministers from our church to come and bless the house and each of us – and Dad hadn't been to church for as long as I could remember. Whether the whole incident really happened our not, he was emotionally scarred by it, and seemed to become a shrunken, scared version of himself for quite a long time after. I never saw or heard from my stalker again.

Jandzmom, FTMB, 2005

BOY INTO DOG

When I was about 11 years old we moved to the small town of Bixby, Oklahoma, and for the first time I rode a bus to and from school. One day as we clambered onto the bus to go home, I idly studied the houses just across the street from the school.

At one house they seemed to be moving, or planning a garage sale, emptying out the attic or some such activity. Furniture, crates, boxes, trunks, lamps, chairs, blankets and every conceivable knick-knack lay out on the driveway, forming a sort of 'U' shape, with the open end toward the street.

Near the inner curve of the 'U', a boy sat on a chair watching the crowd of children disperse along the sidewalks and yards. He sat rather stiffly, with his feet flat on the drive and one elbow propped on a table at his side. He wore dark trousers and a light coloured, long-sleeved shirt.

I kept staring in his direction, more interested at first in the junk than him. I wondered whether or not the homeowners were worried about naughty schoolchildren running up and helping themselves to their property. Eventually, however, I began to think there was something odd about the sitting boy.

He was staring in my general direction, and I noted that his eyes were a weird colour – a waxy brown, almost yellow, clearly visible to me several metres away. No one else on the bus noticed him.

Eventually, the driver climbed aboard and we slowly drew forward. I kept my eye on the weird boy and it seemed almost as if he were changing, his limbs shifting in unlikely directions and his head losing its contours. For a brief, terrifying second, the weird boy's head became – a flop-eared DOG'S HEAD!!

When the bus drew abreast of the driveway, however, it became clear that the stiffly-sitting "boy" was an actual dog – a pointer or something – lying on a table that brought it up level with the back of a kitchen chair. The 'boy's' body had been made of various articles of clothing randomly strewn over the chair, which had looked like trousers and shirt, arms and legs, to me.

What particularly struck me, in retrospect, was how hard I tried to make my eyes still see a boy after the bus started moving – not to mention the creeping feeling across my scalp as the 'boy' seemed to change form even as I watched.
Michael D Winkle, Owasso, Oklahoma, 2006

Strange Visions

9

"You must be seeing things" is a common reaction when someone reports having caught a glimpse of something 'out of this world', whether it's a vision of a traditionally religious nature – saints, angels or the Blessed Virgin Mary – or the appearance of something that just shouldn't be there, like a giant, hat-shaped object or a moving bush covered with tiny lights. In cases like these, can we trust our own eyes?

HEAVENLY SIGHTS

VISIONS OF MARY

My mum says my sister saw the Virgin Mary when she was little. My grandad was very ill in hospital and we were all worried. My mum went to tuck my sister in one night and my sister said, "Don't worry about granddad – the lady said he would be alright." And in fact, he did get well. When my mum questioned my sister about the lady, she was told the lady wore blue and had been standing by my sister's bed.

The thing is, my mother had had her own experience. She had found it hard to conceive after having me, despite receiving treatment. She prayed to Mary and one night, when she was at her lowest, she looked up at the picture of Mary and St Bernadette and she swears the picture of Mary smiled at her. About a week later she found herself to be pregnant with my sister. She believes that she was actually already pregnant when she saw the Virgin's picture smile, and that Mary was telling her not to worry and that a child had already been sent to her.

My sister saw the lady in blue again recently. She was standing by her bed, as before, and said, "Don't worry, she will be safe with me." This was just a few days before my grandmother died.

Whyteowl, FTMB, 2001

ANGEL CONTEST

In the summer of 1998, I was a patient in a psychiatric hospital in Macclesfield, Cheshire, suffering from schizo-affective disorder. Amongst my memories of the rather strange things that happened to me there, the following incident stands out.

One day I was standing by the window of my room looking out and up towards the sky. In one of the clouds I could see what looked just like the faces of two angels. One of them was in a white part of the cloud, with a kind of calm but determined look on its face and directly beneath it in a grey part of the cloud was the face of a scowling, angry-looking angel, being chased by the "white" angel. I am not talking about the outline of the cloud making shapes; these faces were within the cloud itself but distinctly visible. Nor was the illness I was experiencing of the kind that created hallucinations. In my differing episodes of mental illness (1987–1988 and 1997–1999), I have never hallucinated. Furthermore, a female patient in the same corridor, also a Christian, told me she had had a similar experience. I have noticed during my times of mental illness that my mental facilities are somewhat altered to enable me to have what could loosely be called "spiritual" experiences that I do not have when well.

I wonder if atheists, Muslims, Buddhists etc. have similar experiences and if so, what do they see? The Bible mentions warfare between good and bad angels. See Daniel chapter 10 verse 13.

Richard Muirhead, Macclesfield, Cheshire, 2010

THE BABY'S ANGEL

When I was a very tiny baby, my grandmother believed that I saw an angel. I was quite poorly and had an intolerance to baby milk. I was in constant pain and losing weight, and they feared for my life.

One night, my grandma was nursing me, and as usual I was crying. Suddenly, I looked at a spot in the corner, by the ceiling. I stopped crying and a most beautiful smile radiated from my face. I can remember the sensation of seeing a most beautiful face and feeling an incredible sense of peace. My grandma said that she was convinced I had seen an angel. From that time on, my condition improved, and I was soon thriving.

Now, we own a field in North Wales where visions of the Virgin Mary were apparently seen in 1997 and subsequent healing has taken place; there are still occasional claims of people having been cured in mind, body and spirit.

Here is a poem I wrote about my encounter with the angel.

No words, just sensations,
The infant too tiny to speak,
Not too young to feel discomfort,
Of a colicky distended belly.
Feeling the rocking motion
Of the soothing adult,
Trying to ease the child's pain.
Suddenly the baby looks up,
Focusing on the ceiling,
Or are her eyes looking beyond
The reaches of time and space,
Looking into the bright vastness
We believe to be Heaven?
A shining, shimmering light,
A beautiful, wonderful face,
Calm, peace and all pain gone.
A sweet angelic smile
Lights up the infant's face,
Gently she falls asleep,
Dreaming of the baby's angel.
Rose-Mary Gower, by email, 2001

SKY TABLEAU

Recently I was talking with an elderly black gentleman about strange phenomena and he told me something that happened to him when he was growing up in Brooklyn, New York. He was standing on the fire escape of the family apartment talking to his nextdoor neighbour, an elderly woman, when suddenly he saw people in the sky interacting with each other. They appeared to be from biblical times because of their costumes. He said the colours were so vivid and it was just like looking at a page from a Bible storybook. When he pointed it out to his neighbour, she was frightened and ran inside. He called to his family to come and see, but by the time they arrived the vignette had faded away.
Greg May, Orlando, Florida, 2009

SEEING THINGS?

INCONGRUOUS VISIONS

After reading Jung on archetypes and visions connected to the collective unconscious, I was reminded of three very vivid experiences from my childhood. Firstly, in 1965 when I was four years old, my father and I were laying some hardcore prior to concreting a garden path, when I saw a large snake moving quickly between the broken bricks. It had greyish white scales and a large, solid diamond pattern on its back. My father, an ex-police officer, has no recollection of this and says I imagined it, but although I lived at that address for seven years and I would struggle to remember my bedroom, the memory of the snake is absolutely vivid.

Secondly, about seven years later, I was staying at my grandfather's house in Goole, East Yorkshire. I walked along a path next to some allotments, where there were some old rainwater tanks used for watering the plants. Something made me look in one and I saw a reptilian animal about 18in (46cm) long, similar to a baby alligator, swimming in the water. I watched it for a minute, and then, being a normal 11-year-old, I decided to catch it. When I returned with a net and bucket, not only could I not see the reptile, but I couldn't be sure which water tank it had been in. I remember feeling extremely confused, because it seemed that everything had moved from where it was before.

Thirdly, at about the same time and also in Goole, my grandmother and I were walking along a street of houses that had been demolished. The site was flat earth with piles of bricks, roof tiles, old timber and so on. Standing among this debris was a strange hat-shaped object, about 15ft (4.6m) wide and 10ft (3m) high. It was absolutely pitch black, totally non-reflective, like looking into a pitch-black room. My grandmother made no mention of it, and I just looked at it in passing and went on my way.

These three experiences were all visions of something totally out of place, and yet I accepted all three as being normal. I don't recall any feelings of fear or shock. It is only looking back that I realise just how weird they were.

Steven Michael Howe, Rotherham, South Yorkshire, 2008

ALL LIT UP

On 30 September 2009, I was staying in a lodge on an estate near Lockerbie in Scotland. It was a fine evening, and at 6.30pm I was walking in light, mixed

❝ It appeared to be a small bush covered with twinkling white lights ❞

woodland on a hardcore drive that led to the main house. As I rounded a corner I saw, about 50 yards (46m) away and in slightly fading daylight, what appeared to be a small bush, say four to five feet (1.2 to 1.5m) high, beside the drive. It was covered with 50 or maybe more twinkling white lights, like those on a Christmas-tree. I approached it gingerly, even thinking it might be something sinister, but after I had gone only a few yards it slowly turned and faded away into the wood-land and disappeared. The whole incident lasted less than a minute and when I reached the spot there was no trace of the bush or what could have caused the lights.

Do you have any idea what I saw? I was quite sober and in full command of my senses at the time.

Richard Harrison, Sutton, Norwich, 2010

DANCING POINTS

When I was a small girl of six or seven I could, as I understood it, "see air". By this, I meant that I could see dense little dancing points of light in all empty spaces if I adjusted my way of looking in a very small, unspectacular way. These dancing points were particularly visible in the dark. I took them completely for granted, but on mentioning them to an adult one day and getting a dismissive sort of response, they disappeared and I forgot about them.

They returned a few years ago. Without any kind of strain, I can see these "dancing points" of light everywhere. They are in no way unpleasant or strange. They feel very familiar, and on closer examination have a different character depending on where I see them. In underground stations or modern shopping centres, for example, they are rather fuzzy and dull. On a recent visit to London, however, staying in a hotel in Bloomsbury, I observed them one night and noticed that they were well defined, varied and compelling.

Sometimes I have wondered if there's something wrong with my eyes, but now in my mid-40s, I have perfect vision and have never needed glasses. The appearance of the dancing points is exactly as I remember them being as a child. Is it possible that I can see the ether? Or the souls of the departed? Or can I in fact "see air"?

Lise Cribbin, Munich, Germany, 2011

PRAM TURNS A CORNER

A friend and I witnessed the following bizarre event when we were in Marland Hill Primary School in Rochdale, Lancashire, in the early 1990s. The main entrance was surrounded by a concrete football pitch and a descending grass verge which, after a wooden fence, led onto Roch Mills Crescent. The day and time escape me – presumably sometime in the afternoon after lunch – but I do remember that both of us were standing on the edge of the football pitch by the grass verge overlooking the Crescent. I can't recall what we were discussing, but it must have been important to me as despite my friend's desperation to have me look across the road I wouldn't stop talking and do so until he swore at me. While the event didn't last very long, I remember time seeming to drag as I tried to make sense of it.

When I turned to look at Roch Mills Crescent, I saw an old-fashioned blue pram, the material ripped and worn, its hood raised, moving rapidly down the middle of the road. My first instinct was to look for the mother who was presumably chasing after it, but there was no one on the road, leaving me worried that the pram and its presumed occupant would crash into the curb at the end of the road, causing a nasty injury. However, as the pram reached the end of the road, it quite smoothly turned the corner and carried on out of sight.

This ludicrous and surreal event left us strangely unnerved and played on our minds for some time. What now seems odd, aside from the obvious, is that no one else on the football pitch appeared to have seen it. Secondly, the tattered nature of the pram makes me think that it was a vintage one, unlikely to have been in use around 1994. Lastly, it was the stillness of the street that gave the whole incident an eerie feeling – as I said, no one was around on the street to have either pushed or chased after it.

My friend and I have had irregular contact in subsequent years, but each time we meet the story is mentioned by one of us just as a way of validating that we did see this and that one of us hadn't made it up. I did think for a while that it might have been a prank, a remote-control pram as it were, but this seems as fantastical as something paranormal. I mean, why go to so much trouble to rig a pram with a remote control only to try it out on a quiet road with only school-children to act as gullible rubes? I would love to hear of any other "paranormal pram" stories if they're out there!

Michael Byrne, London, 2011

10 The Shadow People

In some ways resembling ghosts or other more traditional figures of the supernatural realm, the unnerving – and often downright menacing – Shadow People (as many have labelled them) are a relatively new phenomenon. Reports of these mysterious entities seem to have been on the increase in recent years, and here we present a small selection from the many distinctly creepy accounts we've received.

THE SHADOW CROWD

About six years ago I was staying at a friend's house. Her parents were away on holiday and weren't comfortable with their daughter and her younger brother being alone for the week.

One night I was asleep on the sofa in their front room, having a very peculiar dream (about a squirrel being in my bedroom!), when I suddenly jerked awake with a feeling of absolute terror. Sharing the room with me were about 20 'shadows'. They looked like the shadowy silhouettes of people you'd see if you were standing in almost total darkness and sense, as much as actually see, someone else nearby. There were two armchairs in the room, in each of which one of these shadowy figures was sitting, and in front of me there was a large crowd of them, sort of milling about as if they were watching something interesting and talking amongst themselves. If you imagine standing in a shop window at Christmas while a crowd of people are looking in at something, that's pretty much how it felt. But although they seemed to be talking, I couldn't hear anything, as if the volume was turned down on the scene.

Friends I've told write the whole thing off as sleep paralysis, but I was propped up on one elbow, blinking and looking away and back again, in full command of my faculties. I stared intently at the middle of the crowd and they seemed to fade out until I could see a line of light where the curtains met; but only the middle of the crowd faded, the rest stayed solid. I'm usually fairly level-headed and not easily frightened, but I experienced a feeling of total terror; they weren't behaving in a threatening way, but I've never been so scared in all my life.

I eventually managed to jump off the end of the sofa (I wasn't going to get off normally as I would have been moving closer to them; they were only about 5ft (1.5m) away and nothing could have made me approach them) and hit the light switch. When I looked back, the room was completely empty. I slept the rest of the night with the light on.

The next day I was thinking about the incident – I hadn't told my friend about it, as she can be quite nervous – when something hit me. It makes the whole thing sound like a tall tale, but I swear to God it's true. The night before had been 24 September – a year to the day from the night I suffered a serious spinal injury (C2 cervical fracture – in other words, a broken neck). I'd recovered with no problems, but the doctors said that if I had suffered damage to the spinal cord that high up it would have killed me outright. The injury had happened at about 4.20am – the same time that the 'shadows' had appeared the previous night. I remember checking the clock before getting back on the sofa to see how long I had to stay in that room on my own.

I can't help feeling that I cheated death and that, a year later, 'someone' came back for me. I certainly felt in fear of my life. I know the whole thing seems incredible, especially with the broken neck 'twist', but reliving it as I write this, my flesh is creeping.
Anon, FTMB, 2004

HAROLD AND THE HAT MAN

I have a close friend named Harold. We have known each other for about 30 years. He and I, at one point, had some very strange encounters with the Ouija board; although the following experience had nothing to do with our Ouija experiences, I mention it as being illustrative of the fact that Harold and I have had more than one shared paranormal experience. When we were first introduced by a mutual friend, it was as though we had known each for years. We have always been very close. The paranormal encounter that I consider the most frightening of my life was also simultaneously experienced by Harold, in slightly different form, but with the major elements of the experience coinciding.

About 25 years ago, while I was living at my parents' house, I awoke one morning to see my bedroom door opening. Immediately, I thought, with distinct clarity, "My father is coming in to empty the trash can." As the door opened

" I became aware that someone dangerous was about to enter the bedroom "

more widely, and I didn't see my father enter the room, I realised that something else was going on, and I began to panic, thinking someone had broken into the house. I believed myself to be fully awake, not dreaming.

As I became increasingly aware that someone dangerous was about to enter the room, I also realised that I was lying on my back and could not move. I then saw a black two-dimensional, shadowed outline of a man in what appeared to be a pointy-looking trench coat and pointy, rimmed hat enter the room.

I have never been more frightened in my life. I somehow knew, as the figure made its way towards me in the bed, that it was going to do something to my neck and kill me. Along with the paralysis, this thought was excruciatingly horrific. As the figure, the most malevolent feeling thing I have ever experienced, got to the side of my bed, near my neck, I 'woke up'.

The room, as I looked around, was just as it had looked moments before during the 'dream', with shadows and early morning light exactly as I had 'seen' them moments before. As bad as the experience was, I filed it under 'nightmares beyond all nightmares' and pretty much forgot about it.

About a week later, I went to visit Harold, who had had a string of bad things to endure. His father had died during the previous year, his mother had run over his cat, and he had been fired from his job. His older brother, going through a divorce, had moved in with Harold and his mother. During my visit, Harold mentioned that he'd recently had a horrible dream. He said that one morning he'd woken up and thought his brother was coming into his room "to borrow some socks". But he soon realised that it was not his brother opening the door, but some malevolent entity determined to kill him. I said, "Stop, Harold. Was it a shadow type thing with a pointy, trench coat-shaped body?"

"Yes," said Harold, "With a pointy kind of hat on." Harold had also been unable to move as the thing came around to the side of the bed, and he had also felt it would do something to his neck.

During the discussion, we both remarked how the ideas about my father emptying trash and his brother borrowing socks just kind of come into our heads as complete thoughts that were almost too placating, especially since my father never came into my room to empty my trashcan and Harold's brother never entered his room unbidden, let alone to borrow some socks.

We both agreed that it was terrifying. We've never talked to anyone else with a similar experience although, since then, I've come across references to the Scandinavian myth of 'the Hag', a succubus-type creature that somewhat mirrors the paralysis and fear elements of our experiences.

Name witheld, by email, 2004

MR NOBODY

I must have been about seven or eight years old when I was walking with my mother near our home one day. I became aware of a man walking parallel to us on our right, and keeping pace with us. The thing was, it wasn't a man, it was a silhouette of a man. There was a trilby-style hat on his head and it looked as if he had on some kind of long overcoat. The silhouette had the appearance of the images you see if you close your eyes and apply pressure to your eyeballs, but quite dark. I told my mother about him (she didn't see anything) and after that I used to call him 'Mister Nobody'. I never saw anything like this again, but what stuck in my mind was that this was a strangely two-dimensional figure.

Caroline -, by email, 2003

CHURCHYARD SHADOW-MAN

I was recently taking my 14-month-old daughter for a stroll in her buggy through a rather nice, peaceful country graveyard near where I live. It was a bright, sunny afternoon with only a light breeze blowing. I was rounding the chapel of rest at the end of the graveyard when I became aware of a black figure to my left and slightly behind me, apparently following me. It was what looked like a two-dimensional 'shadow-man' against the chapel wall, with a crooked hat and long, fluttering cloak or coat. It was very dense black, and resembled a silhouette or a cutout. I paused, as it was creepy, and tried to see if it was me making the shadow on the wall – although as it was a warm day I wasn't wearing a hat or coat. The shadow man 'skipped' out of my vision when I did this. Coincidence or not, a blast of cold, strong wind appeared out of nowhere.

I continued walking, a bit spooked but more curious as to what was making me 'see' the shadow 'following' me. I only got a bit more scared when I left the chapel and carried on walking away; I 'felt' that it was still following me down the path and out of the churchyard, treading just behind me in a malicious way. I was reminded of those stories about the mischievous Puck character who used to play with his unsuspecting victims to scare them when alone. I paused once more to look back, but again just seemed to glimpse a tall black figure, and just as quickly as it was gone again.

I certainly walked out faster than I came in!
Elvira, FTMB, 2003

THE GLASTO SHADOW
Several years ago I used to live on Chilkwell Street in Glastonbury in a very old house. One day I walked upstairs to the bedroom. The door was open, and as I reached the top of the stairs I saw appear from the corner of the room, as if from nowhere, a person-shaped shadow. It looked exactly like a human being but it had no features, as it was as black as the ace of spades. It seemed to be aware that it had been seen and disappeared right in front of my eyes. I saw it again two weeks later, but this time there was a red tint where its eyes would have been. I've done some checking on shadow people and I know that others have seen them as well. Some think they are ghosts, aliens or demons. I'm not sure.
Martin Gidlow, FTMB, 2009

ME AND MY SHADOW
About 10 years ago I had a friend staying for a short time. One night he was on the phone to his girlfriend while I was sitting in a chair facing the door to the hall. I saw a 6ft (1.8m) -tall, jet black figure walk past the door. It looked as if someone had cut a person out of black paper, although it walked like a real person. I thought it must be my then husband going to the bathroom. I got up and looked, but he was still asleep in bed and no one was in the loo.

About four years later, something similar happened. It was about 11pm on a hot, humid night when I couldn't sleep and so was doing odd chores to tire myself out. As I was about to go into the hall I saw what I can only describe as a figure which appeared to be an outline made up of a white line – as if someone had been outlined in tape! It was walking towards the bedroom and my first thought was that someone had got into the flat. I searched the place, but there was no one there. To say it freaked me out would an understatement.

Yesterday, I couldn't sleep and was sitting at the computer. It was about 2am and I was wide awake. Out of the corner of my eye I became aware of a dark figure standing in the hallway. It didn't have a clear edge to it, and I was convinced that I was just seeing things – but I could *feel* that there was someone there and kept looking up into the hall. After about 10 minutes, the figure seemed to have moved right next to me and was generating coldness. I was still convinced I was seeing things, but it didn't go away even when I turned my head to look at 'it'. After a short period it moved behind me and cast a shadow over the area where I was sitting, as if someone was standing over me, between the main light and myself. I kept turning around to look, but it would have been impossible for someone to get past me without me seeing them. After 10 minutes or so it lifted, and the shadow just vanished. I was spooked, but not freaked out.
WH, Dartford, Kent, 2009

THE BLACK DEVILS
In 1985, my family moved to Watertown, South Dakota, a small town 16 miles (26km) away from the Sisseton Reservation. We were tired of living in a cold house in winter, of hauling water or melting snow to cook or wash with. We moved into a small trailer court that had six or seven trailers side by side on the west end of town, only a block or two from the Big Sioux River, which runs through town.

As a Sioux family of four, we were aware of the spiritual side of our Indian heritage. In our culture, people sometimes speak of spirits, which are called Wanagis. In the stories, some of these spirits are good; some are very bad. Some of the spirits are visible, like the pale ghosts in most ghost stories. But some of the spirits are not meant to be seen. They hide themselves from the living.

I still get chills when I think about what I saw one evening in that trailer court. The memory haunts my dreams. What I saw was not meant to be seen. I think the spirit forgot to hide itself from me.

It happened during early evening, the time before dusk when shadows start to darken before nightfall. I remember that the sky was beautiful – afire in red, orange, and yellow. It was a spectacular sunset. I was just getting ready to go cruising with my older brother and two friends. We were all past 18 at the time. My old Chevy was parked behind the trailer house. We had just finished tuning it, replacing the spark plugs, the distributor cap, the points and rotor, the wires, and so forth.

Two trailers down from ours, two women and a man were arguing in front of their trailer. They were so loud that we could hear everything they said. I reached down by my front tyre to grab a ratchet from the toolbox, and I caught a movement out of the corner of my eye. What I saw startled me.

I froze. I can't exactly describe what I saw. A small black thing was walking down the grass trail behind the trailers. That's the best way I can explain it. It was maybe 3ft (90cm) tall with skinny legs and arms. It had a faceless head, and it walked like a human. But it didn't look like a ghost or anything. It was black, as if there were a hole in the air, as if it were a nothingness swallowing light. I've never seen such complete blackness since.

I don't think it noticed me. I watched in astonishment as it walked up to a tree about as big around as a coffee can and put its arm around the trunk and stood there, watching the people who were arguing. I couldn't believe my eyes. The thing was so black that it looked as if the tree had a black hole in it. It seemed to be enjoying itself.

Maybe it liked anger; maybe it brought anger.

All this happened in a couple minutes. One of the other guys said something to me, and I snapped out of my trance.

"What the hell is that?" I asked quietly, pointing at the thing, still standing behind the tree.

Then I threw the ratchet at it, and the thing jumped and spun its head around. I had surprised it. I don't think I was supposed to see it. I think it forgot to hide itself. We ran into the trailer and never saw it again, except, like I said, in my dreams.

Some of the people I've told the story to say it was a water spirit; some say it was a bad spirit, an evil one. Maybe it was what Lewis and Clark referred to as "black devils". I don't know what it was.

Maybe it's best I never know.

Robert L Owens, Sioux Falls, South Dakota, 2012

(As told to John Smelcer, scholar of Native American studies)

11 *Vanishings*

From everyday objects that disappear from the face of the Earth only to return just as suddenly and mysteriously as they departed, to a curious shop that seemed to vanish into thin air and an observatory that could never be found again; these are just some of the many letters we have received which suggest that the world is not quite as solid and predictable as we'd all like to think...

GONE, BUT NOT FORGOTTEN

THE SECOND OBSERVATORY

John Reese was 70 years old when I met him in Ligonier, Pennsylvania. I knew him for 10 years until he died in July 1990. John was a half-blood Shawnee Indian. His father was full blood Shawnee. His mother was Welsh by way of Tasmania. This "incident" occurred during the summer of 1972.

John liked to make any situation as dramatic as possible. Had he been the lone witness, I would have taken the tale with a grain of salt. There was another witness, however: John's wife Ethel. Ethel was level-headed and pragmatic, and whenever her husband would start telling some of his outrageous stories, she'd say, "Now, John!" trying to rein him in. John Reese told this story to me, more than once. Ethel Reese told this story to me, more than once, when John was absent. The story never varied no matter who told the tale. The details never changed. I have to believe the story is true, although I have no explanation for the event.

If you look at a map of Pennsylvania, Route 30 runs from Philadelphia through the Allegheny Mountains to Pittsburgh. Sixty miles (96km) from Pittsburgh, westbound Route 30 passes through Jennerstown, into the woods, over the top of Laurel Mountain, out of the woods, through Ligonier to Chestnut

Ridge and beyond.

John and Ethel owned a small retail shop that accommodated the summer tourists travelling through the Laurel Highlands along Route 30. The shop was located in an isolated spot on the south side of the highway at the eastern foot of Laurel Mountain. Along with the usual Pennsylvania Dutch tourist merchandise, John, through his contacts with the artists of the Tribes across the country, sold American Indian art and jewelry. Business was conducted downstairs. John and Ethel lived upstairs. The shop was called "The Quemahoning Indian Post".

One quiet weekday afternoon during the early summer, John was working the shop alone. Ethel was upstairs in the apartment. The front door opened. A man, a woman and a child walked in. The parking area in front of the shop was hard-packed clay covered with gravel, so any time a car pulled in John could hear the gravel crunching. John was surprised when the three customers walked in, because he hadn't heard a car on the gravel. The three were well dressed, not the typical tourist types. The man was wearing a new three-piece suit. The only items out of place were his well-worn black boots. They'd seen a lot of miles.

John said "Hello". The customers smiled and slowly wandered around the shop. Ethel came downstairs.

After a few minutes, the man walked over to John. "Are you John Reese?" he asked.

"Yes, sir, I am," answered John. "What can I do for you?"

"I was told you'd be able to help us," said the man. "We arrived from Europe a few days ago and we'll be living in this area for some time."

"Whereabouts?" asked John.

"I'm an astronomer," the man said. "I worked in France for the past four years. I've accepted a position here in Pennsylvania. I'll be running the observatory on top of Laurel Mountain."

"So, where are you going to live?" asked John.

"On the ground floor of the observatory," the man answered.

"Are there living quarters in that observatory?" John asked. He had seen the University of Pittsburgh's observatory on Laurel Mountain. That observatory had no living quarters at all.

"Yes," said the man. "From what I've been told, there's more than enough room for the three of us."

"The observatory on Laurel Mountain?" John asked.

"Yes," said the man who was puzzled that John seemed puzzled.

"You've been there?" John asked.

"Not yet. We're on our way there now." He pulled an index card from his pocket and read: "Take Route 30 west to the top of Laurel Mountain, turn left onto Summit Road, and go south past the ski area and into the State Forest. Stay on Summit Road. The observatory will be on the right, the west side of the road. It's visible from the road. A gravel driveway leads to the entrance. The building is white with the living quarters on the ground floor."

John didn't know what to say. The University of Pittsburgh observatory is on the east side of Summit Road, not the west, and it's brown, not white. John had been on Summit Road the week before and had seen no sign of a second observatory.

"I didn't know there was a second observatory on the mountain," he said at last.

"These are my directions," replied the astronomer. "Why don't you and your wife come up for a visit one of these evenings? We'll have coffee and you can see the place."

"Yes," said the woman, who hadn't spoken until then. "That would be very nice. We'd love to have you visit."

"And then you and I could speak privately," added the astronomer.

"We couldn't impose on you," said John trying to be polite, although he did want to see this unknown observatory. "You haven't moved in yet."

"I've been told that the living quarters are furnished and the kitchen is stocked. We just need to hang our clothes in the closet. Please, you and your wife are more than welcome," said the astronomer.

"If you're sure, then we'll stop up. When should we…" John began as he heard a car pull into the parking lot outside.

"Any evening is fine," said the astronomer. "Just drop in. We'll be expecting you."

The front door of the shop opened and four or five people walked in.

"Well, we'd better be going," said the astronomer. "So, we'll look for you one of these evenings."

"One of these evenings," said John.

The astronomer, the woman and the child walked out the door.

"Who were they?" Ethel asked John.

"I don't know," said John. "He never gave me his name."

"There's no observatory on the west side of the mountain," said Ethel.

"I know," said John. "I have no idea what the guy is talking about."

"How did he know your name?" Ethel asked.

"He didn't say," said John.

"What do you think?" said Ethel.

"Beats me," said John. "I guess we'll have to go up and take a look."

Two days later, Ethel and John took an evening ride on top of Laurel Mountain along Summit Road. They drove past the ski area, which was on the west side of the road as always, and they drove past the University of Pittsburgh observatory, which was sitting on the east side of the road as always. They drive on. About a mile past the Pitt observatory they came upon a second observatory, which was sitting on the west side of the road. The second observatory hadn't been there the previous week. John and Ethel turned into the driveway and drove up to the entrance. Then they sat in the car and looked at the building. The sky was clear. The Sun had not set. The observatory was real. The observatory was there. The observatory was white. The ground floor was a very homey looking living space; and on the top of the second floor sat a big dome. John looked at Ethel. Ethel looked at John.

"Do you want to go in?" John asked, finally.

"Not really," said Ethel.

"Neither do I," agreed John. He put the car into reverse, backed out onto Summit Road and headed home.

Ethel and John talked about the second observatory over the next few of days. They couldn't understand how it had gotten there in such a short space of time. They hadn't heard of any construction being done on the mountain, but then they hadn't seen any signs of recent construction at the observatory. They decided to drive back up and take a second look and to knock on the door. So that evening, they drove back up the mountain, back along Summit Road, past the ski area, past the Pitt observatory and another mile or so to the second observatory. But the second observatory wasn't there. The building was gone. The driveway was gone. There was no sign that a structure of any sort had ever been there.

John and Ethel walked through the undergrowth to the site of the second observatory. They stood knee deep in the fiddlehead ferns looking at each other. The vegetation had not been disturbed. Not one fern was bent, not one rhododendron branch was broken.

They returned to the car and drove the entire length of Summit Road. Only the University of Pittsburgh observatory was visible. The second observatory had disappeared into thin air. They went home.

The next day, John went up the mountain; the Pitt observatory was there, the second was not. A week after that, John went up the mountain again but there was still no sign of the second observatory. He drove up and down Summit Road. As he was going past the Pitt observatory for the third time, he noticed a car parked next to the building and three men standing next to it. He pulled in behind it and rolled down his window. The three men walked over. They were in their late thirties and early forties. They didn't look too friendly.

"You looking for something?" asked one of the men.

"Yeah," said John. "I'm looking for the other observatory."

"This is the only observatory up here old man," said the first.

"Baloney," said John. "I was here last week and there was another observatory – about a mile south of here. It was white."

"You're imagining things, old timer," said one of the other men. "There's only one observatory up here, and this is it. So, why don't you just run along home where you'll be safe?"

"Why don't you shove it up your ass," growled John as he put the car into reverse.

A month later, John took some Seneca Indians he knew up the mountain. The Seneca were expert trackers. They searched. They never found any sign of the second observatory.

John couldn't explain it. He kept looking though. Every month or two he'd drive the length of Summit Road in all kinds of weather from clear to rain to thunderstorms to fog to snowstorms. He never saw the second observatory again.

John told me this story in 1982. I asked him if he regretted not knocking on the door of the second observatory when he had the chance. He said that the feeling of "strangeness" was so great on the first visit that he wasn't about to knock on the door. He said that he was comfortable with that decision.

I lived in a chalet, just off Summit Road on top of Laurel Mountain, four miles (6km) north of the University of Pittsburgh's "Airglow" Observatory, from 1984 to 1986. I kept a lookout for the second observatory. I walked Summit Road two or three times a week in all kinds of weather, but the second observatory never reappeared. I live in Ohio now. But anytime I travel through Pennsylvania, I make a detour to Laurel Mountain and Summit Road. When I find the second observatory, I'll knock.

David C Redic, Ohio, 2009

THE OLD CURIOSITY SHOP

It was June 2002 and my wife and I were visiting a friend in Edinburgh. We were walking down the Royal Mile looking for a specific occult shop, which turned out to be closed as the proprietors had gone to a festival in London. We were walking back up the Mile when we were drawn to an antique shop, the window of which was filled with intriguing silver artefacts, such as chased chalices, candlesticks and lovely dishes and platters. Inside the shop was no less amazing, as there were silver objects piled high all around us; the effect was of an enchanting Aladdin's Cave. The interior was of dark wood, dim and dusty. It was a most unusual establishment with a smell like old incense and quite unlike any shop we had ever been in.

Suddenly, a man appeared from behind a pile of silver, presumably the owner. He had silver hair and a long beard and wore black trousers, a dark red waistcoat and a white shirt. He carried a dark wooden staff topped with silver. He greeted us and invited us to look around. I asked whether the staff was for sale and how much it was; he said it was and named the price. It was only the fact that we would eventually be travelling back to England by train and the staff would have been too cumbersome that led to our failing to purchase it. We left the shop with great regret as there were many things which would have graced our home temple. Altogether it was a shame we did not buy when we had the opportunity, as we were never to see this shop or its eccentric owner again. We walked the length of the Royal Mile later that same week to no avail – the shop had literally ceased to exist.

Guy Reid-Brown, Tunbridge Wells, Kent, 2012

WHERE'S THE OVEN?

In 2000, a friend of mine was getting a new oven installed in her kitchen in Geelong, Australia. She purchased one and arranged for a tradesman to deliver and install it. The day he came around, my friend was off work for the morning, but had to go to a meeting that afternoon. When she told me this story about a year later, she admitted to me that at the time, she was angry and impatient for no particular reason, but I think waiting for the tradesman to finish the job had made her angrier. But anyway, she left the front door open, so he could take the old oven out on the trolley to the front yard.

However, not realising this, he took the oven out to the back yard, only just managing to get it down the back steps by himself. She came out and told him

" It was a most unusual establishment with a smell like old incense "

off for bringing it that way. His truck was completely blocking the driveway, and he had to go through the house with the trolley to get the new oven from the back of his truck. She went back into her bedroom, which is next to the back yard, and in her anger, silently wished "for this guy and the stupid old oven to just go away". Moments later, there was a knock on her bedroom door, and the man asked her if she had moved the old oven from the backyard. She had not been out there, but when they both looked, the old oven had gone.

The man searched everywhere, even over the high fences, taking note all the while that there was no way for the oven to leave the yard without the help of a trolley, or three strong men to carry it. There was no one else in the house at the time, and anyway they had heard nothing. The tradesman was freaked out, while my friend didn't care. It didn't seem to shock her, but, as she has been a witch most of her life, strange things are not uncommon for her, and while her family has a gift for being able sometimes to predict death, it makes me, and her, wonder about what other talents she has. The man left quite quickly after that, but called a week later to ask her if the oven had mysteriously 'turned up'. She just laughed until he hung up. Later on she was looking for a casserole dish and her daughter admitted that she had left it in the old oven with some chicken casserole still in it. So whatever 'planet' the old oven is on now, it still has a chicken dinner in it.

Tania Poole, Geelong, Victoria, 2006

LOST AND FOUND

EMAIL LOST IN SPACE?

On 27 April 2003, I got an email from a friend telling me about a radio programme about my area. However, I missed the programme, because when I looked at the date of my friend's e-mail, it was sent on 20 February 2003! This ties in with the programme broadcast, and on checking his PC, my friend found its date setting was correct, and he obviously hadn't resent an out-of-date email, which had already been deleted anyway. Whatever happened to that e-mail in the intervening 10 weeks? What kind of e-liminal experience has it gone through?

John Billingsley, Mytholmroyd, West Yorkshire, 2003

REAPPEARING REMOTE

I recently bought a new laptop computer (Dell XPS M1530), which came with a rather nifty remote control which plugs into a slot on the right-hand side of the machine. Two weeks ago, the remote suddenly disappeared. I turned my flat inside-out trying to find it, but to no avail. After a week of searching, I gave up and tried the tactic of asking out loud for it to be returned, as various people writing to *FT* said this gave positive results. I didn't really hold my breath! Tonight I switched on the laptop and was amazed to find the remote inserted back in its slot in the laptop. My hair stood on end!

Danny Cogdon, by email, 2009

DISAPPEARING TAPE MEASURE

I had an interesting disappearance/reappearance recently. I live with my boyfriend, and he was looking to buy a house. He always took his tape measure with him to measure rooms. At one house we went to check out together, he handed the tape measure to me and told me to go measure something. We got home later and realized that neither one of us had it. I figured that I'd left it at the house, so I went back and looked around for it. It wasn't there, so I came back to our apartment and looked around, thinking maybe he set it down somewhere. The first place I looked was obviously the cabinet he keeps his tools in. I took everything out and then put it all carefully back. Not seeing it, I decided to buy him another one, a larger one. Anyhow, couple days later he says, "Where did you find my tape measure?" I told him that I hadn't seen it, and he opened the door of his tool cabinet, and sure enough, the two were sitting side by side, the smaller and

the larger. He said he just opened the door and it was there. We are the only ones who live in the apartment, the cabinet was locked, and I can't think of any reason that he would be lying about it rather than just saying he found the damn thing (plus he's always been honest with me about everything).
K Cowles, Santa Barbara, California, 2004

SPEC SWAP

Prior to moving to London from Coventry in November 2003, my partner and I had a few experiences of things going missing around the house only to "reappear" where we'd already searched, or sometimes in a place where we thought it was impossible for the item to be. When we moved these occurences more or less stopped.

Last Sunday, my partner, myself and our 21-month-old son went down from London to Fontwell Park races. I don't drive so was in charge of navigation. I wore sunglasses on the way as it was very sunny, my usual specs were in a case in my pocket. At the races I kept my sunnys on all day except for a period of about 15 minutes when it clouded over.

On the way home I reached into my pocket to get out my everyday specs as it was getting dark. There weren't in my pocket and I was annoyed that I must have put them down somewhere. It also meant I would be inconvenienced as I could not see through the sunnys as it was dark and minus specs I am somewhat worse than Mr Magoo.

After stopping to eat I put my hand into the pocket thing on the door at my side of the car and lo and behold the specs case was there. Nothing unusual – I must have slipped it in there after leaving Fontwell. After all this preamble, here's the strange bit: the specs in the case were not the ones I had been wearing when we left in the morning, nor at the races, but a spare pair I have at home. The case was definately the one I had with me all day, it is quite battered and the hinge is bent and as a clincher a different colour from any other case I own. I am at a complete loss as to how my specs swopped places; I say swapped, but I haven't found the others yet, and wonder if anyone has any theories.
Anon, FTMB, 2004

TELEPORTING INHALER?

My son goes to university in a nearby town and lives with friends about 12 miles (19km) away from us. A few days ago I saw on the table, in full view, my son's

inhaler. He hadn't visited for several days and it had certainly not been on the table a few minutes before when I tidied up. This seemed very strange and we could make no sense of it. A few minutes later I spoke to my son as I was meeting him for lunch and he rang to confirm arrangements. He also asked me to bring his spare inhaler as his had gone inexplicably missing. He had it with him and it had suddenly just disappeared. "I can't understand it, it was just here on the table...." I checked to see if the spare was in the drawer where it should have been and there it was.
GC Marks, Yorkshire, 2003

THE MAP CAME BACK

In 1995 I was a passenger in my friend Catherine's car as we drove round Wiltshire looking for crop circles. I had been navigating by means of an Ordnance Survey map of the area, which I'd used on previous visits. On the back I'd drawn sketches of various crop circles that I'd entered, and small crosses on the map itself to indicate their positions. We parked the car next to Silbury Hill, I put the map by my feet on the floor of the car, and we got out, locked up, and climbed Silbury Hill.

When we got back, the map had vanished. Nothing else was disturbed or missing, and the car showed no signs of a forced entry. We emptied the car and searched thoroughly. No map. Later that day we did the same again. Still no map. When Catherine got home to London, she searched every nook and cranny of the car, but still no map. She used the car for the next six months. Then one day she was utterly gob-smacked to find the map, in plain sight on the floor where I had originally left it!
Tim Mayne, London, 1999

DUPLICATED NEEDLES

I had broken my last needle on my Singer sewing machine some months before and needed to do some upholstery work on a chair, but kept putting it off. One Saturday I finally went to buy a package of replacement needles. I walked two blocks to the fabric store, then discovered that there were several different sizes and kinds of needles depending on the model of sewing machine. I returned home, wrote down the model number, went back to the store and bought a package with about 10 needles in it. I returned to my apartment and put the package on my kitchen table.

Before I got down to work I took the garbage from the kitchen downstairs and emptied it in the dumpster. It had grown dark by now and as I turned to walk back upstairs I noticed a yellow package lying near the dumpster in a shaft of light. The area was very clean and no other debris was lying about. When I looked closer I noticed it was the package of unopened sewing needles I had just bought. I thought, "Damn, they must have somehow slid into the garbage can before I took it out of the apartment. I could have easily thrown them out just now".

I took the package upstairs and was about to throw it on the kitchen table when I noticed the original package of needles lying there. They were exactly alike, same model number, same size, identical. I retraced everything in my mind and can't figure out what happened. But if I had taken my garbage out to the dumpster before I walked over to the fabric store then I would have found the needles and would never have had to buy them.
Mark Martin, Austin, Texas, 2003

CHINESE PEN
My partner bought a new radio, which I thought I ought to mark invisibly against possible theft, but didn't get around to it. A day or so later, I found a curious pen – which had come open in my pocket and which I had never seen before – made by Pairdeer, a Chinese firm (as I learnt from an Internet search). It had a battery and transistors in it, but I can't understand why. It also had a plastic point instead of a nib, which wouldn't write; it might be for invisible marking. But finding it in my trouser pocket, that's the really queer thing! My partner had never seen it before either.
David Gamon, by email, 2008

BUTTON FROM BEYOND
One day about eight years ago when I lived in Somerset, I found on the kitchen floor a small button of the sort used on a shirt or blouse. I thought it had come off something of mine, but when I looked, no buttons were missing. At the time I had a few committee meetings and work parties at the house, so I checked with everyone who had been in the house. No one claimed the button, so it went into the button box.

Two or three weeks later, I found a larger button in the conservatory, the sort that might have some off a cardigan – not mine. The same investigation produced no owner, so it went into the button box. After another short time, I found a man's overcoat button on the floor of the least used bedroom. No gentleman had been in the bedroom, and certainly not in an overcoat. The room had been vacuumed, so it was very curious. Nothing further occurred and I decided that if someone was trying to tell me something, they had given up, finding me too obtuse.

Barbara D McCann, Eyam, Hope Valley, 2000

THE SECRET LIFE OF OBJECTS

This is the LEAST frightening fortean experience you will ever read about. Still, it's something that I haven't been able to get out of my head, even 12 years later:

I was 20 years old, and had just moved to New York City. I considered myself a goth/grunge rebel back then, and was busy trying to sow my wild oats after a repressed New England childhood. I lived in a tiny, grungy studio in the Village with very little in the way of possessions or furniture, which was fine with me.

Anyway, at some point, strangely, I began to think about creamers – you know, those little cups with spouts that you use to pour milk into your coffee. I would see them in stores or restaurants and I would want one, badly. I couldn't figure out why; I wasn't the sort of girl to own something as precious as a creamer; no one I knew used a creamer; I couldn't afford to spend money on stupid things like creamers; hell, I didn't even drink coffee or tea!! Yet every time I saw one, it would hypnotise me for a second. I seriously considered swiping one from a cafe or diner, it was that bad.

So after a couple of weeks of this nonsense, I was doing the dishes when I lost a ring down the drain. I turned off the water, grabbed a wrench, went under the sink to try to take apart the drainpipe. That's when I spotted something white behind the pipe. On closer inspection, it was the handle of a coffee cup or something. I grapped it and pulled. The object came out with just a little tugging. YES, IT WAS A CREAMER! It had been lodged behind the pipes under my kitchen sink all that time!

I was dumbfounded. It was nothing fancy, not antique, just a cheap, faux-porcelain creamer. The bottom said it was from Woolworth's.

How the heck did it get there? A previous tenant of the apartment, obviously, but why jammed behind the pipes? Had it been calling out to me for rescue in some way and that's why I kept thinking about a creamer? Do objects DESIRE to be used? I know humans often invest prized possessions with a certain amount of energy or power – hence "haunted" objects, voodoo dolls, and the uncanny ability of teddy bears to ward off monsters. Had this cheap-ass creamer been much beloved by its previous owner, and some residual energy was drawing me?

The theory I find most plausible is that I subconciously saw the creamer one day while I was fetching something from under my sink, and the whole creamer obsession was my brain's way of reminding me it saw something. Then again, maybe I should just consider it a little gift from the gods.

Just gets me thinking about the secret life of objects. For example, a friend of mine recently told me how she stayed home sick from work one day only to witness (while hiding in a closet which she bolted when she heard the front door unlock) that the old guy with Tourette's Syndrome who lived next door had been letting himself in with the spare key she kept under her doormat (dumb, I know) where he would proceed to strip to his underwear, walk around the apartment, and touch all her things (even petting the cat!!!) When the police later apprehended and questioned him, she learned that this had been going on every day.

Makes you wonder what goes on in your house while you're out.
Sarah Goodwin-Nguyen, New York City, 2004

12 *Poltergeist!*

At what point does a common-or-garden haunting become
a poltergeist case? Is it when objects are moved around,
thrown across rooms or rearranged in strange patterns?
Is it when disembodied moans and mysterious bangs wake
the household on a regular basis? Or, perhaps, in some
unusually violent examples, where physical harm is inflicted
on the human focus of these unexplained energies?

POLTS IN THE HOME

A PECKISH POLT?

On the evening of 4 January 2005 I was relaxing in front of a film in the living
room of my eighth floor flat. At about 8.30 I clearly heard the fridge door slam
shut in the kitchen (the next room). Assuming it was one of my young daughters,
I paused the DVD and got up to investigate. There was nobody in the kitchen.
Both my daughters were fast asleep a good 10 metres (33ft) away in their
bedroom and my wife was having a shower. Even if somebody had sprinted to
the fridge, I would have seen and heard them pass the open double-doors of the
living room.

Our fridge door closes with a very distinctive rattling thud and could not be
mistaken for the neighbours' front door, a car crashing, a bang from upstairs etc.
Furthermore, we live in Russia and in January all the windows are sealed shut
against the intense cold. This rules out any draughts or air currents. Our fridge
door, if left ajar, tends to swing fully open and stay in that position. It takes some
force to slam it closed so that it is audible from another room.

A sceptic might have put the incident down to auditory hallucination, in spite
of the fact that I was sober and not particularly tired. If it had happened just
once, I might have come to agree.

Two evenings later I was once again watching a film in the living room. At 8.30 I heard the distinctive sound of the fridge door crash shut. I leapt up and ran to check where everybody was. My daughters were asleep and my wife was watching TV in bed. I told her what I had heard and she helpfully told me to "stop being ridiculous". So I quickly walked back to the kitchen. This time the kitchen door itself was closed. In nine years of living in our flat I have never seen that door in any position other than fully open. There is no way it could have closed itself, not to mention the fridge door as well. A closed kitchen door barring one's way is no hallucination but a very real chunk of wood. So who or what closed the fridge and kitchen doors?

A hard-nosed sceptic who says that any incident must have a 'rational' explanation, but who doesn't properly look at the facts, is voicing an opinion just as arbitrary as a believe-it-all occultist who claims invisible pixies were responsible. I suggest that if something cannot be explained using information we already have, this does not mean it will not at some point be explained. So-called supernatural phenomena may well have 'rational' laws governing them that are waiting to be discovered and which will be accepted by the science of the future. Meanwhile, I'd like to ask if it could just be possible that my fridge door was closed twice by a peckish poltergeist.

Oliver Jarvis, Obninsk, Kaluga Region, Russia, 2005

SPOOKED IN EDINBURGH

In 1979/80 my wife and I rented a friend's flat in Edinburgh. It consisted of the ground floor of a Georgian house in the New Town district, large and quite grand. I found it slightly creepy the first time I stayed there alone. Then my wife Gabbi and Benson, my large Irish Setter, came up north. First Benson refused to enter the flat, then when I dragged him in, he was clearly uneasy and kept looking over his shoulder and refused to be left alone.

One night Gabbi and I were fast asleep when all the lights suddenly came on in the hallway outside our bedroom. I leapt out of bed, assuming we had intruders; all the lights had been turned on in every room, but there was no trace of a living soul. I searched for an open window, or any possible way that someone could have entered, but there was none. It gave me a very strange feeling and the hair stood up on the back of my neck. Benson was terrified and refused to sleep in the hall where he usually slept and insisted on spending the rest of the night with us.

During the couple of years or so we had the place, similar things happened quite often. Lights went of and on by themselves, objects moved when we were out and there was a very strange feeling generally. I had the electrics checked for any short circuits, but there were none and in any event, each time it happened, the light switches had always been physically moved. By this time, our friends had moved abroad, so I never had the opportunity of asking if they had experienced similar unusual events in the flat before they rented it to us.
Donald Crighton, Branksome Park, Dorset, 2004

COMPUTER POLTS?

My girlfriend sent me an email asking me out for a treat on my birthday. I didn't receive it, even though I've received all her other emails. However, she got a reply from my email address, dumping her. Only, I didn't send it. It was tricky to talk my way out of this. I just wondered if any *FT* readers have had any similar experiences, or if they can explain what happened. The message was almost in my style – a good imitation – but not quite right, with errors of syntax I wouldn't commit. I've ruled out anyone using or hacking into my computer, and so I have to resort to more supernatural explanations. I don't think I had any unconscious desire to dump the girlfriend, which my computer obligingly picked up telepathically and acted on. The girlfriend, on the other hand, is very psychic and a bit on the witchy side, but in a good way. But she'd scarcely ensorcell my computer to send her a message, dumping her – unless she's trying to tell me something (which she isn't – I checked). However, she did, shortly after this, receive an email from a friend, accepting a lunch invitation, which she, the girlfriend, hadn't sent – even unconsciously or in her sleep – because she doesn't like this person. I suspect a sort of cyberpoltergeist – a mischievous, mildly malignant, trivial nuisance, as polts so often are.
Patrick Harpur, Frampton, Dorset, 2009

STOKEY POLT

Many years ago my girlfriend and I lived in a squat in Stoke Newington, London. The house was Victorian and in fairly good shape and we shared it with about eight other people we knew; they said that "strange" things happened in the house that they couldn't explain.

As we were going to sleep on our first night there my girlfriend experienced a weight on her chest and could not move, as if someone was sitting on her. At the same time I heard whispering, sometimes barely audible and sometimes as if it was right next to my ear. We spoke about this the next morning and decided to move our bed to the opposite side of the room. When we did this, it stopped.

Where I worked at the time we were issued with a six-zone yearly travel card; because of its cost, I used to always keep the card safe. One day it went missing; we turned the bedroom upside down looking for it, but it was nowhere to be found. I reported it lost and was gearing myself up for having to pay for a replacement. About three weeks after losing the card I fell ill and decided to stay at home. I was lying in bed, watching my girlfriend iron her clothes for work. She was doing this on the floor, using a towel to iron on. When she was finished she picked up the towel and my travel card was underneath!

Another couple living in the house with us told us of an episode that happened to them. They were sharing a bath and Steve decided to shave. He needed to change his razor blade and as he was fitting the new one he dropped it in the bath. They were obviously worried about being cut so they both stood up and looked in the bath - but the blade had disappeared! They drained the bath, but still no blade. They checked with a second blade to see if it could fit down the plughole, but it clearly could not.

Another housemate reported waking in the middle of the night to see a young girl standing outside the third floor window!

The house has now been redeveloped and I wonder if the current residents experience anything out of the ordinary.

RS, London, 2001

PARANORMAL ACTIVITY

My parents' house in Rickmansworth, Hertfordshire, has been subject to infrequent paranormal activity for over 20 years now, mainly falling into the category of 'Gremlin' incidents. A couple of the more interesting ones are the day my mother was using the vacuum cleaner when it suddenly stopped working. While looking at the more obvious causes, she opened up the plug leading to the power lead and found that all the wires had been mysteriously reversed. Another incident occurred with an old handbag belonging to my mother. This bag's handle was a thin gold chain which broke one day, so my mother consigned it to the bottom of the wardrobe. Clearing out the wardrobe one day, months later, she retrieved the bag and found that the chain had been miraculously and invisibly repaired – it was good as new! These events have become so commonplace as to become part of family lore, more a topic of family news than anything else – stories to entertain my wife and me on our visits home.

Activities over the last six months or so, though, seem to be of a very different order. One day in April of this year, my mother phoned me to report the following incident. She had been clearing up after Sunday lunch, when a heavy old ornamental shield mounted on the wall of the kitchen came crashing down all by itself, knocking a bottle of wine onto the floor and smashing it. She cleared up all the bits save one: she could not find the neck of the broken bottle, however hard she searched for it. Three weeks later, she walked into the kitchen and there it was, right in the middle of the kitchen floor.

A few weeks after this my father, who is retired, was working in his study alone at the top of the house, sometime in the mid-afternoon. As he was working, he distinctly heard the voice of either a woman or child saying repeatedly "Hurry up! It's six o'clock! It's six o'clock! Hurry up! Tee hee hee!"

It says a great deal about my dad, and his lack of fear (or imagination), that he stayed in the room all the time the voice was chanting, and looked out of all the windows, to see if there were kids in the next door garden, or in the road outside. There were not, so with the voice still chanting, he started looking behind filing cabinets, book cases and so on for the source of the noise. Eventually, he called my mother, but by the time she arrived the voices had stopped. This happened another two or three times over the next couple of months, and has not been heard since.

Then, in August, my mother was working in the house, transferring food into our spare fridge in the garage. She put the food in without incident, closed the door, and went back into the kitchen. She then remembered that she needed to turn the fridge thermostat down, so she went back and opened the fridge door to do this, and found the lower shelf of the fridge covered in shards of glass. These had not been there five minutes earlier.

The last event, also from around this time, occurred when my father was watching TV in the kitchen, and he saw a glass of water slide across the kitchen table, completely of its own accord.

I should say that I have not experienced any unusual activity in the house myself… until last weekend. Taking advantage of my parents' regular trips abroad, I was down at the house with my wife and a group of 10 friends to celebrate 5 November with a fireworks party. To be accurate, this took place on the 6th, which was a Saturday. After the fireworks, the party continued indoors.

In spite of the roaring fire, a few people complained of feeling cold as the evening progressed. I gave this little thought until afterwards. At one point my wife was taking pictures with her digital camera of a couple of guests dancing. She succeeded with one picture, but the next one took so long to frame up and light (in digital photography terms) that she was left with an empty frame, composed of an empty chair, with a painting above it, and no people. After taking this shot, she sat next to me and asked me to look at the camera display as there was a fault with the picture. We showed this picture to everyone in the room, and all agreed that, instead of an empty chair that no one had sat in all night by the way, there was a tapering column of oily black smoke rising out of the chair. I have seen photos of paranormal activity before, and I was convinced that I was looking at something wholly unearthly. The chair had been completely empty, and the two people dancing were nowhere near it.
Anon, FTMB, 2004

HARASSED BY SPIRITS

A MYSTERIOUS ENERGY

We've been living for five years in a very old house in France, in a small village next to Paris, called Orgeval. We were renting the house, and we just loved it. We had been living there for approximately a month when my mother started having disturbing experiences. She seemed to become the target of a 'spirit' or 'energy', possibly because was the person who spent the most time in the house. It seemed to want to drive her crazy, or to make her very frightened.

She never saw anything – just lights going crazy, extremely cold winds in the house (it was August), the feeling that something was touching her bed sheets at night, sounds of footsteps on the upper floor, and so on. This energy was simply harassing her constantly. She started thinking that she had gone crazy, because none of us ever said anything about having weird experiences. So she decided to keep it for herself, hoping it would come to an end.

One day my grandfather – who unfortunately could no longer understand what was happening in everyday life – said that he was so cold, because there was so much wind in the house. He asked my mother to close the windows. It was warm outside and the windows were already closed. At that point, my mother knew she was not going crazy. She got extremely angry (nobody wants to see her angry!), and not even knowing whether this 'energy' could understand her or not, she started yelling: "I know you're there! I know it's your house, not ours. But we're living here now, so please let's share it. You let us stay here, and we won't bother you – we can all live together."

After that, things started getting better. My mother told us about the presence, and, some time after, we also started having similar experiences. But it no longer seemed aimed at making us leave – it was just a sort of 'contact'. Every time I felt the presence, I was scared, although I never felt in any danger.

This energy was almost always there (although from January to June, its presence was not so constant; I have no idea why) and almost every night I could feel it touching my sheets, or I could see it 'playing' with the lights. It (I don't know whether it was a he or a she) even tried to communicate: once, my mother had left some fresh nuts on the floor of an upstairs room to dry out. A week later, she went up to the room and noticed something weird: the nuts had been arranged in a funny shape over the floor. Reading a book some time later, my mother discovered that this shape was the sign of a neighbouring village. Could this have been the village where the spirit was born?

Anyway, the whole experience changed my life. Before moving into this house, I didn't believe in life after death. Now I know that, in some cases at least, it happens. The 'energy' in our house, for instance, was in some way conscious – it knew what it was doing. It knew when I was getting too scared, and would immediately leave the room where I was. I had the feeling, every time, that he or she was very sad.

Once, as I was going to bed, I saw a huge amount of light coming through my bedroom door. It didn't have a shape, but it was incredibly powerful. It stayed in front of me for some seconds, and it was too much for my young mind. I panicked. I didn't know what to do. I couldn't move or speak, and the light was so bright it was hurting my eyes; I had to focus all my energy on my breathing, just to be able to continue with this simple task. When I couldn't handle it anymore, the energy left, and went upstairs. I couldn't find the courage to follow it, which I still regret today. This was the only direct 'sighting' I had, and – again – apart from my fear, it was mostly a great sadness that I felt. Perhaps that was just me projecting, but I have no doubt there was a real consciousness there. And that's what scares me: the possibility of having a conscious existence after death, and the possibility of suffering for an undetermined period of time.

We later learned from the people of the village that every other family who had rented the house had moved out after three to six months. The owners had tried everything to get rid of the spirit, or whatever it was, without success, and were just hoping that it would disappear at some point. Once, they even hired somebody who claimed that the house was built on the tomb of an ancient soldier; we were even told that someone else had once seen the shape of a man on a horse in the garden. I don't know if all of this is true, I just know what we experienced, and that's enough.

I was relieved when we left, but now I miss this presence and I wonder what's happening in the house. I have heard that the family who rented it after us left after eight months.

Daniela – , by email, 2002

MY SISTER'S POLTERGEIST

My sisters and I have been the subjects of hauntings for as long as I can remember. Right now, my concern is for my youngest sister. When my parents moved from their home of 25 years, about four years ago, I thought she would be free of the entities we suffered growing up. But I've been proven wrong.

I've experienced very little since moving to the new house – some rustlings in the night, voices and groans (some of which my mother and I heard together), but nothing that would really alarm me after having lived at the old house. The activity now seems to happen around my 16-year-old sister. Light bulbs have been known to shoot from their sockets around her. Lights will either turn on and off in her presence, or at times will refuse to turn off when she hits the switch. If it was strictly an electrical problem, you'd think after four years some-one else would have had the same thing happen to them, but no, it's just her.

Glasses have shattered in her room, shoving themselves forcefully off shelves or off her dresser. She'll wake up in the morning with deep scratches and bruises on her back and legs. The bruises I could possibly explain away, with her being a heavy sleeper and sometimes rolling into the wall in the night, but the scratches throw me. She has a horrid habit of biting her nails down to nubs... by some stretch of the imagination (and considering the length of her nails, it'd be a big one) I might see the scratches on her legs as being possibly self-inflict-ed, but not down the middle of her back – sometimes a continuous scratch from between her shoulder blades to the small of her back.

" She'll feel someone in the room with her, or staring at her, or see shadows "

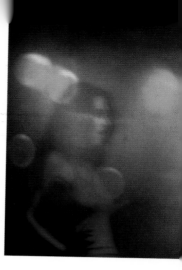

In the old house, as well as the new one, she's been more prone to 'seeing' whatever it is around her than myself or our other sisters. She's seen white mists and dark mists that will hover for a moment, then dash through a wall.

She has other things happen that are less frightening and which we're quite accustomed to. She'll feel someone in the room with her, or staring at her, or see shadows moving around. One time, while she was washing dishes, she stepped out of the kitchen for a moment and came back to find all the plastic cups out of the cabinet, stacked in a pyramid shape. No one else went into the kitchen behind her -- she would have seen – and no one really had time to take the cups out and stack them in such a fashion.

I wouldn't be concerned about these things accept that whatever it is around her seems to have some violent tendencies. I'm going to ask her to keep a journal of her moods and the goings-on in the house to see if negativity from herself has any significance to the happenings around her. The ghosts of the old house were mean and cruel, but at least we were never outright attacked, or had anything thrown directly at us. They seemed to exist more on mental anguish.

I'm thinking possibly these things are coming from somewhere within herself, somewhat like a poltergeist. I don't feel it's anything that's followed her over from the old house, as it's not their style. Perhaps something new has taken a 'liking' to her? Something from within her? What do you guys think?
Anon, FTMB, 2004

13 The Twilight Zone

> You could be forgiven for thinking, after reading the letters and posts contained in this book so far, that the avenues of the anomalous had been well and truly trodden. You'd be wrong, of course. When we've sorted the premonitions from the poltergeists and the time-slips from the teleportations, then we're left with the *really* weird stories. Welcome to the Twilight Zone...

WEIRD OLD LADIES

STRANGER FROM A NIGHTMARE

As a child I lived in a North Yorkshire village with my parents and grandmother. At this time I used to occasionally have a reoccurring nightmare in which I would be alone in the house, playing in my bedroom with toy cars. Suddenly, I would hear 'kitchen' noises from downstairs such as pots and pans bashing, cutlery being shuffled and so on. This in itself was scary, as I was supposed to be alone. I would gingerly edge to the top of the stairs absolutely petrified, call out for my grandma and sit on the top step. Eventually, I would hear someone walk from the kitchen and then appear at the bottom of the stairs – I expected it to be my grandmother, but it wasn't. Instead, it was a very plain looking middle-aged woman I had never seen before. She would simply stand at the bottom of the stairs, look up and grin at me. I would start screaming, and then usually wake up. It doesn't sound particularly scary now, but to me it was terrifying.

Eventually my family moved away from the area, but shortly before we left my mother took me to the village fete. It was just the usual small village gathering with a few stalls and a marquee. Towards the end of the day my mother engaged someone in conversation about us moving away and they introduced her to a friend of theirs who was planning on moving into the village. To my horror it was the same woman who had stood at the bottom of my stairs in my night-mares! She didn't say much, if I recall, simply smiled and then moved away – but I swear she looked at me knowingly, as if she too had seen me somewhere before. I was at the age where I didn't question it that much. I just felt uncom-fortable and wanted to go home.

Ever since that day, I have always put it down to coincidence – however I can't help but wonder if the woman from my nightmares ever ended up living in my old house...
Anon, FTMB, 2004

LADY IN PURPLE
Approx 17 years ago, when I was 18, I went to visit my sister for the weekend. She had moved to Liverpool and this was my first visit. She was living in a ground floor flat in a large old converted house. The flat was very cold, had lots of old furniture and a boarded up fireplace.

We went out on the Saturday night a couple of pints at her local and were back home by 11pm. There was only one bedroom in the flat, and it was too cold to sleep on the couch so I shared the double bed with my sister.

I dropped off to sleep, and dreamed. In my dream, I woke up needing to pee (as you do after a couple of pints), and so got up and walked to the bathroom. I pulled the light switch cord, but nothing happened and the light did not turn on. I pulled and pulled, but it wouldn't budge. I had to go in the dark, but, fearing for my aim, I decided to sit down on the toilet. As I did so, the bathroom door swung open and a middle-aged woman walked in. She was dressed in purple, had purple hair and in her hand she had a large kitchen knife. She walked towards me with the knife raised.

Before she could reach me, the bathroom was invaded by what I can only describe as small, pudgy cartoon dinosaurs, which seemed to scare this woman away. That's when I woke up, needing to pee for real this time.

So, I got out of bed, went to the bathroom, pulled the light switch... but noth-ing happened. The light did not turn on. I pulled and pulled, but it wouldn't budge. To say I was scared is an understatement, but my needs were great and I managed to do in the dark what I needed to, and got back to bed without further incident. Morning came, and I went to the bathroom. I pulled the light switch cord out of curiosity and the light came on.

My sister asked me to pop out and get a paper, which I did. There is a curving path to the front door of the house, and halfway along there is a blind bend where a large bush obstructs your view. On returning to the house I cleared this bend, only to be confronted by a middle-aged woman dressed in purple, with purple hair. The exact same woman, in fact, who was in my dream!

After taking half an hour to calm me down, my sister said that the woman was her landlady. I must point out that I had never, ever seen the woman before. We talked some more and my sister described other strange occurrences in the flat, including a full bin bag migrating the length of the bedroom during one night.

My sister doesn't live there anymore, but we still talk about the house, and I remember it as if were yesterday. It's not the sort of thing you'd forget!
Anon, FTMB, 2004

THE PREVIOUS OCCUPANT

In 1988, following my parents' divorce, my mum found a new place to live – a fairly average 1960s, three-bed terraced house. We moved in in late July or early August of that year. After a very exhausting day of unpacking and a couple of beers, I went to bed. Sometime towards morning (as I found out when I woke up a bit later) I began dreaming. Someone was at our front door. I opened it, and standing there was a tall, old lady. She had iron-grey hair, long hands, a very light complexion and wonderfully blue eyes. She also had this nervous habit of putting her hands to her mouth. Very politely, she asked if she could come in. I said to her that I'd have to check with mum first, as this was her new house. The old woman very politely but very firmly insisted that it was her house, then practically begged me to let her in. I said again that I'd check with mum, then turned away from the door. In my dream, I felt the hairs on the back of my neck rise – then I suddenly woke up. No more than a dream, I thought, and dozed off again.

Over the next few days, between unpacking and organising the place, we got to know our new neighbours, most of whom were fairly elderly. Over a cup of tea, I asked one of them, Sophie, about the previous occupant.

"Oh, she was a very nice woman," she said. "She died about a year ago. Very dignified, and so polite. She was really tall."
Sophie went on to describe the woman in my dream perfectly, nervous hand gesture and all!

I wonder what would have happened if I'd let her in?
Paul Gallantry, by email, 2004

BAFFLING ENCOUNTERS

BUT IT'S NOT HALLOWE'EN!
One of the weirder incidents I had was just a quick glimpse of somebody pulling out of a mall one day: I could have sworn the person was a classic Frankenstein's monster, with square head and neck-bolts (like the classic Jack Pierce make-up created for Boris Karloff) and was screaming in complete anguish.

I'm sure it's just one of those things that was a trick of the light and my mind trying to create a picture, but it was completely surreal! And, no, it wasn't Hallowe'en, just an ordinary Saturday!

Doug R, Atlanta, Georgia, 2004

"HIYA TREV!"
About 10 years ago a bloke dressed as a giant rabbit waved at me from the other side of the road and shouted "Hiya Trev!" To this day, I don't know who it was. I went home and told my wife who immediately hid the scotch, and the kids haven't stopped taking the piss since.

Anon, FTMB, 2004

PACK OF PEE WEES
Once, as a student in Providence, Rhode Island, I walked down Benefit Street to see an army of people dressed like Pee Wee Herman – from the grey suit to identical Pee Wee Masks. They were marching in twos, about 15 of them, and as we passed them on the other side of the street they turned and stared in unison – and then pointed at us!

ARGHHHHHHH!!!!!!!

Anon, FTMB, 2004

STRANGE DAY IN CANTERBURY
I don't know if this counts as an episode of high strangeness, exactly...

I went to a thoroughly enjoyable housewarming party in Canterbury, Kent, at the weekend. Lots of old friends, good time had by all etc. I stayed the night, and at around four the next afternoon got ready to get the train back to London with about five others. Needless to say, we were all heavily hung over.

The first oddness occurs when, just as we are getting ready to leave the house, a peculiar group of people walk by the window. They all look youngish, in their 20s, and one is wearing a dressing gown. Another is wearing a sort of cape with a Wonderwoman-style headpiece. They all look a bit weird. Probably off to a fancy dress party, of course, but they don't look like they'd made any effort to dress up in coherent costumes; they just look, well, odd.

Our hostess has offered to walk us to the station, so we head out the front door and are walking along the street outside the house, when a woman, accompanied by what I presume was her daughter, shouts out very forthrightly after our hostess by name. Our hostess turns round, but doesn't know her. The woman asks our hostess where a particular car park is. Our hostess answers, and then asks how the woman knows her name. The woman does a sort of fingers-to-her-forehead "I'm psychic" gesture and says "telepathy". She'd probably heard one of us refer to our hostess by name, but still… the way she addressed her as though she was an old friend was, yes, odd.

Then, we're walking up the High Street, with me alongside a friend called Mike:

1) We see a chubby man walking alongside his chubby son. The man has what looks like drinking straws protruding from his nostrils.

2) A couple of young girls (12–13?) walk past us in the opposite direction. As they pass, one of them looks at Mike and shouts "Bolognese!".

3) This happens as we are walking past a closed and empty shoe shop on our left. A shoe in the display falls to the floor and triggers an alarm. Mike and I stop and stare at each other in bewilderment for a moment before carrying on to the station.

Although each incident on its own is far from remarkable, and all could probably be easily explained, the cumulative effect was quite disorientating for everyone involved. We wondered if we were all being over-sensitive because of our collective hangover. It was still odd, though.
James Machin, by email, 2004

TOUGH OLD BIRD

Back in the late Eighties, a group of us were enjoying a skiing weekend at Dufton Youth Hostel in Northumberland. It was December, and had been snowing heavily for a few days, so the skiing was excellent. On the Sunday, most of our group decided to go and ski again, but my friend Frank and I decided to do a walk instead.

We were all experienced high level skiers, walkers and climbers, and Frank and I set out to walk up to High Cup Nick, which might not have been so demanding if the weather hadn't come down so fiercely. We kept agreeing to just go a little further and then turn back. By this time, the snow was knee-deep and the wind was blowing so hard we were almost knocked over, in spite of huge rucksacks and every item of protective clothing you could wish for. We were also in the prime of youth and fitness, and although we knew this could have been a risky climb, given the weather conditions, we were very confident and full of energy.

At last we collapsed in a heap under some overhanging tree roots, and pulled out thermos flasks of hot tea. We were genuinely knackered and were still a little way off the summit. We were just telling each other that we would have to make one last effort or be called cissies when we got back to the group, when into our view bounded a couple of those little wiry dogs that look like lavatory brush heads and usually have bows on their collars. These two didn't, but they were wearing those little tartan 'body warmer' things. Frank and I looked at each other in bemusement and wondered if we were succumbing to delirium or something. Just then a woman's voice, very loud and hearty, was heard shouting, "Hector! Sandy! Here boys – come to heel at once!" and into view strode a lady who it would not be unkind to describe as elderly. She was dressed in a three quarter length quilted gilet, a knee-length tweed skirt, a silk headscarf (probably with horse's heads and bridles on it) and leather lace-up brogues! She strode past us at an amazing rate of knots, pausing only to call to us "Bit nippy isn't it – should be lovely once the Sun's out!" without even sounding out of breath.

Frank and I simply gaped after her retreating back: she might have been walking down the high street in some Cotswolds town. Oh, and did I mention she was carrying one of those rigid shopping baskets?

I thought Frank summed it up well, once the hysteria had subsided. "It was people like her who built the Empire!" he said; and I was forced to agree.
Hecate10, Sedbergh, Cumbria, 2004

...AND THE MAN FROM BURTONS WINDOW
Which reminds me of another puzzling meeting that took place a few years back over an Easter weekend.

I was walking with my husband in the Lake District, along the shores of

Haweswater to be precise. We had decided to re-do a walk we had done a few years earlier along the entire shoreline. It's just about possible to get all the way round, although some of the 'paths' are well nigh impassable in places.

It had been an extremely rainy couple of weeks and we were well prepared for the inevitable mud and bog, had donned waterproofs and waterproof trouser, and all the usual other paraphernalia. Nonetheless, by half way round we were utterly mud-splashed to the eyeballs and beyond. I only mention this because of our meeting further on.

We came to a place where the path thankfully widened out to a comfortable one-person width – we had literally had to hack our way through dense undergrowth for what seemed like miles, and were covered with bits of vegetation, mud, perspiration and flies. Looking ahead, we could see that the path was intersected by a stream and then the undergrowth closed in again. To cross this shallow stream there were some stepping-stones, but the banks were exceptionally boggy for quite a way around it and the stones very slippery and mossy.

We were just about to cross when we saw someone coming towards us from the other side of the stream, out of the forest. He was the only person we had seen since leaving the car park a good couple of hours before and we were about to speak when his appearance stopped us in our tracks. (Bear in mind we were only about half way round the lake. There are no roads and the only way is by the path we were on, which goes over exactly the same terrain as we had covered already).

He was immaculately, and I mean *immaculately*, dressed in a white, open-necked cotton shirt, white linen baggy trousers, with a straw fedora on his head and a silk cravat tucked into his shirt collar. He was wearing light, cream-coloured leather shoes and had a cream linen jacket slung over his shoulder. He was perhaps 60-ish, with fair hair and a pleasant smile. He wished us a jaunty "Good afternoon" as he passed and carried on lightly stepping along the track we had just walked. In a few seconds, he had disappeared and we just stared at each other. There was not a speck of mud, debris or vegetation on him: in fact he looked as if he had just stepped out of Burton's window display!

It goes without saying that we experienced nothing but more mud, bog and dishevelment on the rest of our journey, but puzzling over where this apparition could have come from, a good six or seven miles (10-11km) from the nearest tarmac road, at least gave us something to take our mind off our aching feet!

Hecate10, Sedbergh, Cumbria, 2004

CREEPED OUT

FACE IN THE MIRROR

A weird thing has been happening to me for the past two weeks. Whenever I pass a window or mirror, I see a strange, featureless face just behind my reflection. It's definitely not my reflection – it appears to be behind me, although when I turn to see who is there... there's nobody! I don't see the whole face, only a glimpse, as if as soon as I catch sight of it, it quickly vanishes. All I can say about it is that it appears to have no mouth or nose, just dark eyes. The face is very pale, and a stranger thing is that it has blurry edges, while my reflection is clear. Perhaps I just don't see it for long enough to pick out any features.

My eyes are fine, so this is starting to freak me out.

Skunkimunki, FTMB, 2004

BEHIND THE MIRROR

About 1970, I was 24 and living in a flat in a suburb of Sydney called Eastwood. Something woke me from a dreamless sleep one night – it must have been because the room, which was normally dark at 2 or 3 in the morning, was light enough to see. There was a floor-standing swivel mirror about 5ft 6in (1.7m) high at the foot of the bed, and I had the impression that there was something behind it, a sort of 'shadow', so I got up to have a look. There was a figure there, quite solid-looking and standing slightly sideways, with its eyes unblinking and staring into the corner of the room near the head of the bed. It didn't look aggressive, but had an impassive expression. It was quite a bit shorter than the mirror, I would say shorter than 5ft (1.5m). It had a very stocky build, long matted curly black hair, and an extremely ugly face with a big 'lumpy' nose and bloodshot eyes. Quite dark skin, and wrinkly. I seem to recall its clothing as being a very dirty white in coarse material, something like a hessian smock, and with a belt around the middle.

In the couple of seconds it took me to scream and run to the bedroom door, it had gone. I lived in that flat for about two years and this was the only strange thing to happen there. It couldn't have been a real person, as I was on the second floor and he would have needed a ladder, of which there was no sign. I don't think it was a nightmare, as on first waking up I felt calm – and I hadn't had a drink that day! I have never been able to come up with an explanation, and

" When I pass a mirror I see a strange face just behind my reflection "

neither have I told it to anyone outside my own family.

My husband, who has been laughing and jeering at this story whenever I mentioned it over the last 27 years, has now stopped laughing. In February 2009, when he was staying in a 16th-century hotel in Colchester, he saw a ghost – not once, but half a dozen times. This annoyed him, because he was adamant that no such things existed.

Beryl Goodliffe, by email, 2009

THE THING IN THE BACK OF THE CAR

One of my cousins was driving home from work one night when she heard a rustle in the back seat and suddenly what felt like an icy cold hand gripped the back of her neck. She was too terrified to glance at the rear view mirror to see who it was. She just kept driving.

After several miles she saw a police car on the side of the road, waiting for speeders as they do. She screeched her car to a halt in front of him and pounded on the horn like crazy. When the police officer got out of his car and came over to her window, the hand released her. She sprang out of the car crying hysterically and telling him someone was in her back seat. The officer shone his flashlight into the car and finally opened all the doors and did a physical search. There was no one there. She was still so upset that the officer had to follow her the rest of the way home. She and her little boy were living with us at the time and my mother remembers the officer walking my cousin to the door to make sure she was all right.

J Long, Kentucky, 2004

THE THING IN THE BATHROOM

We moved into our current house on the north edge of Dartmoor about a year ago. It's not an old building, but an ex-council house built in the 1950s. There are apparently several 'things' in this house, including a few grey, cat-sized, slug-shaped ghostly things that creep into the living room from the hall and then leave again when they realise someone is in there (it's not just me who has seen them).

Then there is the 'thing' in the bathroom. I was finding the toothbrushes knocked over, and figured it was the cat, but a few months ago I was taking a shower when a shadow appeared on the other side of the orange shower curtain. It couldn't have been someone coming in, because the door had not opened. The figure looked a bit like it could have been a man, but with very square shoulders. Suddenly the toothbrushes went flying.

This just made me cross, so I shouted at it quite a lot about how they were our toothbrushes and we didn't appreciate them being thrown around the room. It went away and there has been little sign of toothbrush interference since, although I do warn houseguests.

Sam Fleming, by email, 2003

PINMAN AND FRIENDS

I'd like to relate two instances of unwelcome bedroom visitors. The first was when I was about eight and sleeping in the bedroom of a bungalow belonging to family friends. I awoke to see a strange phosphorescent creature standing near the bed, something like a child's drawing of a skeleton, but just in outline without bones or other details. The closest comparison I can think of is the pin-man drawing in The Saint books, which I was then too young to have read. Its head was oval, not round, and as far as I can remember, it had eyes but no other features. As I watched, paralysed with fright, it began to jump up and down as if on springs. At this point, I screamed the place down and adults came running to see what was going on, assuming I'd had a nightmare. To this day I'm sure I hadn't, and of course they found nothing, but I was always nervous of sleeping in that room again.

The second incident happened in 2004 in the back bedroom of the house here in Derby where I lived till quite recently. In the small hours, I awoke as I heard and felt something trying to jump onto the bed. "Get off!" I shouted, thinking it was one of our cats escaped from the kitchen. I gave it a push, then suddenly realised it was much bigger and heavier than any cat. It fell off the bed, then had another go, and I could hear its claws scratching at the bedclothes and wooden bed-frame. I saw something resembling a small bear with a long nose and very thick curly fur. It also had long claws, which it dug into my hand quite painfully. Years ago, there was a cartoon character called 'Flook' in a daily newspaper, and my mystery visitor rather resembled a malevolent version of it. On hearing my description, my daughter said it sounded like an anteater with an afro, which summed it up very well.

I was paralysed with fright at some point during the encounter, but I also remember pushing the thing off the bed and hearing it thud onto the floor. After the third successful attempt to dislodge it, I came to my senses and put the light on. There was nothing there, of course, and later investigation proved both our cats to be still shut in the kitchen. However – and here comes the interesting bit – in the morning I found I had some hefty scratches on my right hand and several fingernails were broken, with one jagged bit of nail twisted round, sticking into my skin. So – was there really something there and did it scratch me, or did I hit the edge of the bed or side of the dressing table first (and if so, why?), then dream up the creature to explain it? I suffer from migraine, but didn't have it on this occasion.

Years earlier, another daughter saw an apparition (which seemed to be the ghost of an old gardener) in the same bedroom, but her visitor seemed quite benevolent. The house was built on a former market garden.
Brenda Ray, Mickleover, Derby, 2008

BEYOND BIZARRE

ATTACK OF THE KILLER TABLE
When I was eleven, my family came into some money and we moved from the housing projects into a new large house. My mother and stepfather bought a bunch of antique furniture to furnish the house, including a round dining table, which apparently had it in for me.

Every time I sat at the table, I would get long red scratches somewhere on my body, usually (but not always) on my arms. The scratches never hurt: they would just appear, and then fade away after a couple of days. They looked like scratches made by fingernails. It took me a while to make the connection that tables equals scratches, it being such a strange thing. I tested this in front of my family members many times and it became a sort of in-joke as to why Hestia avoided the breakfast nook. I did indeed avoid the table and ate in the dining room when everyone else was eating in the breakfast room.

My mother got rid of the table when I was 19, when my sister accidentally dropped a can on it and made a huge deep gash in the tabletop. Our replacement table is very similar but doesn't have the same 'interesting' effect on me. Has anyone else had similar problems with inanimate objects? Any theories as to what might've caused this, even if it was something psychosomatic? Or have I been ready for the loony bin for the past 14 years?

Hestia -, FTMB, 2004

MYSTERIOUS MOUNDS OF FOOD

My husband is on a two-year temporary job assignment in a town some distance from our home. His company set him up in an apartment there. Most weeks I stay with him and we go home on weekends. Three times in the past year a strange thing has happened at our 'home away from home'. I have found some food on the ground just a couple feet from our front door. Ours is the last in a row of townhouses, and the food is always left on the side of the doorway where there is no neighbouring house. It's always a sizeable amount and in a neat round mound that looks as if it was purposely arranged there and not just accidentally dropped. It almost looks like some sort of 'offering'.

On one occasion it was about a dozen whole potatoes, neatly stacked in a pyramid next to our door. The last time it happened, we returned from a three-day weekend at home and found a neat pile of what seemed to be about four cups of the biggest pumpkin seeds I've ever seen in my life. On the first occasions, I didn't give it much thought, just thinking that these weren't the sorts of food one would normally leave out for wildlife. Anyway, it's a busy city street and the only animals I've seen have been stray cats.

It was only after it happened the third time that I started getting creeped out by it. It's certainly possible someone is being a bad neighbour and leaving out food they don't want stinking up their own doorway, or it could be a prank of some kind. I know I probably sound like a kook, but these incidents have caused me to wonder if this is some sort of rite or ritual.

It's very surreal to walk out your door and find a neatly arranged stack of food sitting there, with no apparent explanation.
Leandra -, by email, 2004

SCHOOL WITCH

When I was at primary school in Nottinghamshire in the 1970s I had a teacher who left an impression more vivid than most. It was a very small school with only two classes and this teacher, a young woman, came in to take charge of the lower class, which included me. The first thing she did was to tell us that our soft toys came alive in our bedrooms at night when we were sleeping, and they played and danced around our sleeping selves. We didn't believe her straight away but she was quite adamant this was true and there was quite a serious discussion about it that left one or two of the kids quite awestruck. Not much noteworthy about that, but this teacher definitely had something slightly spooky about her (besides always wearing head-to-toe black, as I recall) that filtered back to parents and gave at least one of my friends nightmares.

Her big impression came at Christmas time. Word went round beforehand that this teacher had something planned for the party. There was a partition between the classrooms that was opened up after lunch one day, and the entire school of about 30 sat on chairs arranged around the edge of the rooms. 'Miss X' sat on the edge of the circle where the classrooms met while the headmaster handed her a long pole that was used to open the catches on upper windows with a brass hook at one end. All the curtains were drawn shut so the room was dim. The headmaster said that she was going to 'catch' spirits. Holding the pole at one end with both hands, she closed her eyes and went into a trance, then started slowly whirling the pole around, calling out to the spirits she was evidently trying to reach. As her 'performance' intensified, the pole hook was smashed against the floor on each quickening rotation, Miss X shouting and working up into a frenzy, seated all the while. This scene of her, with her splayed legs covered by an ankle-length black skirt, rolling her head and calling out as the pole's hooked end smashed against the floorboards is seared into my memory. Of course the kids – and probably the other teachers – had never seen anything like this before, and I can definitely say that I haven't seen anything like it since! The kids were pretty shocked by what was going on, some might have cried, so after no more than a minute of this the headmaster stepped in. The pole was taken off Miss X, the curtains were drawn back, normal festive games resumed.

Unsurprisingly, there was a parental fuss over the episode. Miss X left very soon after and things returned to normal, until the school closed within a few months and subsequently became a tearoom. I went there for lunch recently, and while finding the same floorboards on which our witch teacher smashed her 'spirit hook', wondered what inspired her to do such a thing and what became of her.

Jerry Glover, Leighton Buzzard, Bedfordshire, 2011

Fortean Times would like to thank all those who have written to us, emailed, or posted on the 'It Happened to Me!' forum at the FT website, to share their experiences over the past 39 years. A particular thank you goes to those whose stories appear in this volume:

Neal Allen, Alex -, Kevin Andrew, Jerry B, Paddy Berry, John Billingsley, Suzy Blue, David Bruin, Michael Byrne, Caroline -, Danny Cogdon, John B Collins, Dr Simon, Cooke, K Cowles, Lise Cribbin, Donald Crighton, Ellyn Cummens, Daniela -, Matthew Davey, Alison Derrick, Lynsey Drewitt, Rupert Ell, Elvira, Eric Fitch, Michael Fletcher, Sam Fleming, Paul Gallantry, David Gamon, Martin Gidlow, Jerry Glover, Beryl Goodliffe, Sarah Goodwin-Nguyen, Jay Gourd, Rose-Mary Gower, WH, Doug Hall, Susan Harmon, Patrick Harpur, Richard Harrison, Hecate10, Philip Hemmise, Hestia -, Brian Hopkins, Alan Howard, Steven Michael Howe, Martin Hunt, Ian -, Colin Irons, Jandzmom, Jane -, Oliver Jarvis, David Jones, AK, Duncan Kaiser, Kate -, Jared Keeler, Tracy Kinsella, Elsie L, Piers L, Ian Langdon, Pat Law, Leandra -, Tom Lev, J Long, Barbara D McCann, Bronach McElhone, Adam McGechan, James Machin, Trace Mann, Marion-, GC Marks, Mark Martin, Greg May, Tim Mayne, Tom Morton, MrSnowman, Richard Muirhead, Neil -, Robert L Owens, J Pérez, David Perry, Bernice Policastro, Tania Poole, Susan Price, Carla R, Doug R, Brenda Ray, David C Redic, Colin Reid, Guy Reid-Brown, Rich -, Dan Roach, Lloyd Robson, Laragh Rogers, Jack Romano, Russell -, RS, Sam -, Tony Sandy, Skunkimunki, Steve Small, John Smelcer, Dan Smith, Hayley Smith, Lee Stansfield, Stargazeypie, B Steninger, Sally Thomas, Matthew Thorley, James Laurent Toure, Jeffrey Vallance, Paul Walker, Paul Warhurst, Stephen Watt, Whyteowl, David Wingfield, Michael D Winkle, Taras Young and all anonymous posters on the Fortean Times Message Board (some posters' details were lost in a website changeover some years ago; if you'd like to put a name to any of the stories in this book, then please get in touch so we can credit you in future editions).

Thank you to those who helped make the pictures in this volume happen: David Anderson, Josh Blom, Faith Brandon-Blatch, Arran Brown, Capucine Deslouis, Gareth Gascoine-Leopold, Masha Kolomeitz, Lenka/Capucine/Ivan, Abigail Mason, Ioan Nascu, Ioana Nascu, David Newton, Brandy Row, So High Soho.

FOR MORE REAL-LIFE STORIES OF THE UNEXPLAINED, SIGN UP TO THE *FORTEAN TIMES* MESSAGE BOARD AT WWW.FORTEANTIMES.COM AND VISIT THE 'IT HAPPENED TO ME!' FORUM.

IF YOU HAVE YOUR OWN BIZARRE STORIES TO TELL AND WOULD LIKE TO SHARE THEM WITH US, THEN SEND YOUR LETTERS TO:
PO BOX 2409, LONDON NW5 4NP, UNITED KINGDOM,
OR EMAIL SIEVEKING@FORTEANTIMES.COM / DRSUTTON@FORTEANTIMES.COM

More tales of the unexpected...

The faceless figure that stepped out of the fog

The ouija session that summoned a shadow man

The ghostly children who played patacake

All these stories and more in...

It Happened To Me!
REAL-LIFE TALES OF THE PARANORMAL
VOLUME 4

Ordinary people's extraordinary true stories from the pages of
ForteanTimes

£7.99